D0118021

the **low**-fat cookbook

low-fat, great taste

the **low**-fat cookbook
low-fat, great taste

MURDOCH
B O O K S

USEFUL INFORMATION

The recipes in this book were developed using a tablespoon measure of 20 ml. In some other countries the tablespoon is 15 ml. For most recipes this difference will not be noticeable but, for recipes using baking powder, gelatine, bicarbonate of soda, small amounts of flour and cornflour, we suggest that, if you are using the smaller tablespoon, you add an extra teaspoon for each tablespoon.

The recipes in this book are written using convenient cup measurements. You can buy special measuring cups in the supermarket or use an ordinary household cup: first you need to check it holds 250 ml (8 fl oz) by filling it with water and measuring the water (pour it into a measuring jug or a carton that you know holds 250 ml). This cup can then be used for both liquid and dry cup measurements.

Liquid cup measures

1/4 cup	60 ml	2 fluid oz
1/3 cup	80 ml	2 3/4 fluid oz
1/2 cup	125 ml	4 fluid oz
3/4 cup	180 ml	6 fluid oz
1 cup	250 ml	8 fluid oz

Spoon measures

1/4 teaspoon	1.25 ml
1/2 teaspoon	2.5 ml
1 teaspoon	5 ml
1 tablespoon	20 ml

Nutritional Information

The nutritional information given for each recipe does not include any garnishes or accompaniments, such as rice or pasta, unless they are included in specific quantities in the ingredients list. The nutritional values are approximations and can be affected by biological and seasonal variations in foods, the unknown composition of some manufactured foods and uncertainty in the dietary database. Nutrient data given are derived primarily from the NUTTAB95 database produced by the Australian and New Zealand Food Authority.

Oven Temperatures

You may find cooking times vary depending on the oven you are using. For fan-forced ovens, as a general rule, set oven temperature to 20°C lower than indicated in the recipe.

Note: Those who might be at risk from the effects of salmonella food poisoning (the elderly, pregnant women, young children and those suffering from immune deficiency diseases) should consult their GP with any concerns about eating raw eggs.

Alternative names (UK/US)

bicarbonate of soda	—	baking soda
besan flour	—	chickpea flour
capsicum	—	red or green bell pepper
chickpeas	—	garbanzo beans
cornflour	—	cornstarch
fresh coriander	—	cilantro
single cream	—	cream
aubergine	—	eggplant
flat-leaf parsley	—	Italian parsley
hazelnut	—	filbert
minced beef	—	ground beef
plain flour	—	all-purpose flour
polenta	—	cornmeal
prawn	—	shrimp
Roma tomato	—	plum or egg tomato
sambal oelek	—	chilli paste
mangetout	—	snow pea
spring onion	—	scallion
thick cream	—	heavy cream
tomato purée	—	tomato paste
courgette	—	zucchini

Weight

10 g	1/4 oz	220 g	7 oz	425 g	14 oz
30 g	1 oz	250 g	8 oz	475 g	15 oz
60 g	2 oz	275 g	9 oz	500 g	1 lb
90 g	3 oz	300 g	10 oz	600 g	1 1/4 lb
125 g	4 oz	330 g	11 oz	650 g	1 lb 5 oz
150 g	5 oz	375 g	12 oz	750 g	1 1/2 lb
185 g	6 oz	400 g	13 oz	1 kg	2 lb

Contents

Introduction

This isn't a diet book, but a cookbook of wholesome family meals with reduced fat—delicious alternatives to buying pre-packed supermarket low-fat dinners, many of which tend to be bland, insubstantial and quite expensive. What we've done is taken a selection of popular recipes and looked at reducing their fat content. We certainly haven't wanted to compromise on taste, so if your personal favourite isn't included, it may be because it tastes so great the way it is that a low-fat version would be a poor substitute.

Fat is often portrayed as a villain and we must remember that it is not—everyone needs a certain amount of fat in their body, to help with growth and development and to carry fat-soluble vitamins throughout the body. It is the quantity and type of fat we eat that can cause problems. Foods contain a mix of different fats, but one type usually predominates.

Saturated fats, those that have been implicated in some health problems, are found mainly in animal products, including butter, cream, fat on meat and other fats which are solid at room temperature, like dripping or lard.

Mono-unsaturated fats, which are generally regarded as being better for us, are found in olives, olive oil, many vegetable oils, most nuts, avocados and, in small amounts, in fish, chicken, lean meat and also eggs.

Polyunsaturated fats, found in nuts, grains, seeds and oily fish, usually remain soft or liquid at room temperature.

If you want to limit your fat intake, it is recommended you try to have no more than about 30–40 g of fat per day (30 g for women and small men, 40 g for men and taller women). With this in mind, we have carefully developed a range of recipes that contain less than 15 g fat.

Each recipe has the fat per serve clearly marked, so this will help you keep tabs on how much you are eating. For those who wish to change their dietary habits to eating low-fat but find it hard to accept the idea of giving up creamy sauces to eat plain 'undressed' vegetables or meat, we've come up with some special ideas that won't break the 'fat bank'.

If you are aiming to lose weight, cutting back on your fat intake is a good start and this book will certainly help you monitor that, but you also need to exercise regularly.

Ingredients

As well as using the recipes in this book, once you get used to cooking and eating the low-fat way, you will find many of your favourite dishes don't need to be given up completely but can be adapted by using lower-fat ingredients. The tips on the following page explain simple ways to change your cooking habits and other ways will become obvious when you try the recipes. For example, you can use low-fat natural yoghurt instead of sour cream, or whipped ricotta with orange instead of whipped cream. When frying onions, use aerosol oil sprays and add a tablespoon of water to the pan to speed the softening process. Use fish canned in brine or spring water instead of oil.

These days we are lucky with the choice and variety of low-fat foods available—bread, dairy products including spreads and cheeses, and meat which is sold well trimmed and labelled according to its fat content. The lean pre-trimmed cuts are excellent—they mean you can't be tempted to leave the fat on in a weak moment. Some shop-bought mince has quite a high proportion of fat, so make your own from lean meat or choose the mince labelled low-fat. New Fashioned Pork and Trim Lamb are low-fat cuts of meat.

For cheeseaholics there are many fat-reduced Cheddars on the market but it is worth knowing that other cheeses, such as fetta and ricotta, also have low-fat versions.

Read all the labels on food packaging. These will tell you how much fat is contained in a recommended serving size or in a 100 g portion. If there isn't a nutritional table on the packaging, the manufacturers must list the ingredients in order of the quantities used. If the fat is near the beginning of the ingredients, put it back and try another brand.

Be aware that just because a product is labelled 'light', this doesn't necessarily mean light in fat: it can mean low in salt, flavour, colour and weight, or low in alcohol as in Light Beer. In addition, don't be confused by foods claiming to be low-cholesterol or no-cholesterol—this doesn't necessarily mean low in fat, just low in animal fats. These foods, which may include nuts, nut products, margarines or oils, can still contain a high percentage of other fats. Processed foods tend to be higher in fat. The more natural and less prepared the food, the better it is for you.

Low-fat Cooking Hints

In many of our recipes you will find 'cooking oil spray' in the ingredients list. This is readily available at supermarkets and is a great addition to the shopping trolley. It is simply oil under pressure in an aerosol: no chemicals are added. Sometimes lecithin, a natural preservative and emulsifier derived from egg yolks and legumes, is added to make the oil appear white so that you can see where you have already sprayed. We used it for greasing pans or coating food and found far less oil was needed, as it covers a larger area. For the low-fat cook, this is a must-have.

There are many ways of achieving low fat results, using very little or no fat at all. Investing in a couple of non-stick saucepans and frying pans is a good start. They require only a quick spray with oil, if any, and then you can pan-fry knowing that nothing is going to stick. There's no need to keep pouring in extra oil.

Steaming is a very good alternative to roasting, as it locks in the natural flavours. Add herbs, spices or lemon juice to meat, chicken or fish, or drizzle with sauce, then wrap in foil or baking paper and seal securely to keep in all the flavours. Steam in a bamboo or metal steamer, open the parcels at the table and enjoy the aroma and flavour.

Stir-frying uses a minimal amount of oil to seal meat, and cooking is done quickly and at high temperatures so there is less opportunity for fat to be absorbed. The meat is then usually removed and set aside. When stir-frying vegetables, add a tablespoon of water to prevent them from sticking—this also produces steam which speeds up the cooking process even more. Return the meat to the pan, add any sauces and flavourings and toss well.

Grilling and barbecuing are not only low-fat but produce wonderful flavours. Lightly grease the grill or barbecue with oil spray or brush lightly with oil. If you grill on a rack, rather than a hotplate, fat can run off the meat and be discarded later.

High-fat ingredient	Reduced or low-fat alternative
Milk, yoghurt	• Use low-fat varieties.
Whipped cream	• Use evaporated skim milk and chill before whipping. • Whip low-fat ricotta cheese with icing sugar and low-fat milk or fruit juice.
Sour cream	• Use low-fat yoghurt or buttermilk. • Blend cottage cheese with skim milk and lemon juice or vinegar. • Mix low-fat evaporated milk with lemon juice.
Whole eggs	• Use 2 egg whites or $^{1}/_{4}$ cup of egg substitute for 1 egg. If the recipe needs a few eggs, keep at least one or two whole eggs to maintain texture. Replace 3 whole eggs with 1 whole egg and 4 egg whites. Before you add the fresh egg whites, whisk them slightly.
Cream cheese	• Use low-fat cream cheese or low-fat fromage frais. • Use blended low-fat cottage cheese.
Cheese	• Use smaller amounts of lower-fat varieties. • Choose low-fat ricotta or cottage cheese. • Instead of a Cheddar cheese topping, mix a little grated Parmesan with oats, bran or wheat germ.
Butter or margarine	• Use small amounts of reduced-fat varieties (but not for baking). • Use lower-fat alternatives (chutney, cottage cheese, a little avocado) for sandwiches or only butter one slice of bread.
Oil	• Use less oil or use olive oil spray, stocks and juices for stir-frying or sautéing. • In cakes, replace oil with an equal amount of fruit purée and one-third of the oil—use puréed prunes, dried apricots or apple.
Mayonnaise/salad dressings	• Use non-fat varieties. • Make your own low-fat dressings (vinegar, herbs, lemon juice, ricotta, tomato paste) or sauces (low-fat yoghurt, buttermilk, mustard).
Coconut cream or milk	• Use reduced-fat versions. • Use low-fat yoghurt and a little desiccated coconut.
Pastry	• Use filo pastry, brushing every 3–4 layers with oil, juice, low-fat yoghurt or concentrated stock. • Mix cooked rice with egg white and pat onto a lightly oiled pie dish. Bake before using as a pastry base.
Sweet pie crust or slice base	• Combine plain reduced-fat sweet biscuits or wafer biscuits with dried fruit (apricots, prunes or figs) in a food processor until the mixture forms a ball. For 150 g biscuits, you need 75 g fruit. You may need to vary the amounts depending on the fruit's moisture.
Cakes and biscuits	• Minimum fat needed for biscuits is 2 tablespoons per cup of flour. • Replace oil with an equal amount of fruit purée plus one-third of the oil. • Use non-stick pans.
Meat and poultry	• Buy lean cuts and remove any visible fat before cooking. • Remove the skin and fat under the skin from poultry before cooking. • Keep portions small and fill up with vegetables and legumes.

Better tips for better eating

- Trim all visible fat from meat or chicken.
- Remove any chicken skin before cooking, to avoid the temptation to eat it after it's cooked.
- Use less meat in stews and casseroles. Instead, add lots of fresh vegetables or pulses such as chickpeas or kidney beans instead.
- Increase the amount of fish and legumes in your diet.
- Serve meals with plain pasta, boiled or dry roasted potatoes or boiled/steamed rice to help you fill up with no extra added fats. Remember it's not the potato that puts on weight, but what goes on top.
- Skim stews or soups to remove excess fat or, better still, refrigerate overnight and lift off solidified fat. They taste better the next day anyway.
- Use low-fat plain or skim milk yoghurt in sauces and stews instead of cream.
- Thicken sauces by reducing the liquid and adding puréed vegetables, instead of using buttery sauces.
- Try alternatives to oil for basting and moistening (lemon or orange juice, vegetable juices, mustards, soy sauce, wine or fortified wines such as sherry). Try frying onions in a little of the juice from tinned tomatoes.
- Use stock in soups instead of cream.
- Use light evaporated skim milk as a substitute for regular cream and light coconut milk instead of regular.
- Never, never, never go shopping when you're hungry!

Don't go hungry

Snack on low-fat, high fibre and no-fat foods when the munchies hit:
- Fresh fruit and vegetables (but go easy on the avocado).
- Fresh fruit and vegetable juices.
- Skim milk and low-fat milk drinks; low-fat yoghurt.
- Pasta with tomato-based sauces.
- Steamed rice.
- Baked jacket potato with low-fat yoghurt and chives.
- Home-made muffins.
- Wholegrain bread and bread rolls; bagels; English muffins; crumpets with low-fat spreads such as honey, jam or Vegemite.
- Some crispbreads (read the labels).
- Rice cakes.
- Plain popcorn and baked pretzels.
- Dried fruit.

Recipes

4 g and under

Hokkien Noodle Salad

450 g (14$\frac{1}{2}$ oz) Hokkien noodles
200 g (6$\frac{1}{2}$ oz) broccoli, cut into florets
4 spring onions, sliced
1 red capsicum, thinly sliced
1 green capsicum, thinly sliced
1 carrot, sliced on the diagonal
100 g (3$\frac{1}{2}$ oz) fresh baby corn, halved lengthways
100 g (3$\frac{1}{2}$ oz) snow peas, sliced

3 tablespoons chopped fresh coriander leaves
1 teaspoon sesame oil
$\frac{1}{4}$ cup (60 ml) sweet chilli sauce
$\frac{1}{4}$ cup (60 ml) light soy sauce
2 tablespoons lime juice

PREPARATION TIME 20 minutes
TOTAL COOKING TIME 5 minutes
SERVES 4

1 Gently separate the noodles, place in a heatproof bowl and cover with boiling water. Leave to stand for 2 minutes, then rinse under cold water and drain well.

2 Boil or steam the broccoli for 3 minutes, or until bright green and tender. Rinse under cold water and drain.

3 Place the noodles, vegetables and coriander in a large bowl, and mix well.

4 Combine the sesame oil, sweet chilli sauce, soy sauce and lime juice. Pour over the salad and toss to coat.

NUTRITION PER SERVE Protein 20 g; **Fat 4 g**; Carbohydrate 92 g; Dietary Fibre 8.5 g; Cholesterol 20 mg; 2085 kJ (498 cal)

Smoked Cod and Lentil Salad

250 g (8 oz) brown lentils
1 onion, finely chopped
1 bay leaf
500 g (1 lb) smoked cod
1/4 cup (15 g/1/2 oz) chopped fresh dill
3 spring onions, chopped
100 g (31/2 oz) sweet spiced gherkins, chopped
100 g (31/2 oz) sun dried capsicum, chopped

Dressing
2 cloves garlic, crushed
2 tablespoons low-fat mayonnaise
1/4 cup (60 g/2 oz) low-fat natural yoghurt
2 tablespoons chopped chives

PREPARATION TIME 25 minutes
TOTAL COOKING TIME 45 minutes
SERVES 6

1 Place the lentils, onion and bay leaf in a pan, cover with water and bring to the boil. Reduce the heat and simmer for 25–30 minutes, or until the lentils are just tender. Drain and set aside to cool. Do not overcook the lentils or they will become mushy.

2 Half fill a frying pan with water. Bring to the boil and add the smoked cod. Reduce the heat and simmer gently for 10 minutes, or until it flakes when tested with a fork. Drain and cool slightly. Break into large pieces.

3 Add the dill, spring onion, gherkin and capsicum to the lentils, then gently fold in the cod pieces.

4 To make the dressing, combine the ingredients in a bowl and whisk until smooth. Pour over the salad and lightly toss to coat.

Notes

Smoked cod is available from most supermarkets or fish markets.

You can make this salad up to 3 hours ahead but don't add the dressing until you are ready to serve.

NUTRITION PER SERVE Protein 25 g; **Fat 4 g**; Carbohydrate 25 g; Dietary Fibre 7 g; Cholesterol 45 mg; 1005 kJ (240 cal)

Vietnamese-style Chicken and Cabbage Salad

3 chicken breast fillets
1 red chilli, seeded, finely chopped
¼ cup (60 ml/2 fl oz) lime juice
2 tablespoons soft brown sugar
¼ cup (60 ml/2 fl oz) fish sauce
½ Chinese cabbage, shredded

2 carrots, grated
1 cup (50 g/1 ½ oz) shredded fresh mint

PREPARATION TIME 15 minutes
TOTAL COOKING TIME 10 minutes
SERVES 4

1 Put the chicken in a saucepan, cover with water and bring to the boil, then reduce the heat and simmer for 10 minutes, or until cooked through.

2 While the chicken is cooking, mix together the chilli, lime juice, sugar and fish sauce. Remove the chicken from the water. Cool slightly, then shred into small pieces.

3 Combine the chicken, cabbage, carrot, mint and dressing. Toss well and serve immediately.

NUTRITION PER SERVE Protein 30 g; **Fat 3 g**; Carbohydrate 15 g; Dietary Fibre 3.5 g; Cholesterol 62 mg; 900 kJ (215 cal)

Potato, Broccoli and Coriander Soup

500 g (1 lb) broccoli
cooking oil spray
2 onions, finely chopped
2 cloves garlic, finely chopped
2 teaspoons ground cumin
1 teaspoon ground coriander
750 g (1½ lb) potatoes, cubed
2 small chicken stock cubes

1½ cups (375 ml/12 fl oz) skim milk
3 tablespoons finely chopped fresh coriander

PREPARATION TIME 15 minutes
TOTAL COOKING TIME 30 minutes
SERVES 4–6

1 Cut the broccoli into small pieces. Lightly spray the base of a large saucepan with cooking oil, then heat over medium heat and add the onion and garlic. Add 1 tablespoon water to prevent sticking. Cover and cook, stirring occasionally, over low heat for 5 minutes, or until the onion has softened and is lightly golden. Add the ground cumin and coriander and cook for 2 minutes.

2 Add the potato and broccoli to the pan, stir well and add the stock cubes and 1 litre of water. Slowly bring to the boil, reduce the heat, cover and simmer over low heat for 20 minutes, or until the vegetables are tender. Allow to cool slightly.

3 Blend the soup in batches in a food processor or blender until smooth. Return to the pan and stir in the milk. Slowly reheat, without boiling. Stir the chopped coriander through and season well with freshly cracked pepper and salt.

NUTRITION PER SERVE (6) Protein 10 g; **Fat 0.5 g**; Carbohydrate 20 g; Dietary Fibre 6 g; Cholesterol 2 mg; 580 kJ (140 cal)

Leek and Potato Soup

cooking oil spray
2 leeks, white part only, sliced
3 cloves garlic, crushed
1 teaspoon ground cumin
1 kg (2 lb) potatoes, chopped
1.25 litres vegetable stock
1/2 cup (125 ml/4 fl oz) skim milk

PREPARATION TIME 20 minutes
TOTAL COOKING TIME 45 minutes
SERVES 4

1 Lightly spray a large non-stick frying pan with oil. Add the leek, garlic and 1 tablespoon water to prevent sticking, then cook over low heat, stirring frequently, for 25 minutes, or until the leek turns lightly golden. Add the ground cumin and cook for a further 2 minutes.

2 Put the potato in a large pan with the leek mixture and stock, bring to the boil, reduce the heat and simmer for 10–15 minutes, or until tender. Purée in a processor or blender until smooth. Return to the pan.

3 Stir in the milk, season and heat through before serving.

NUTRITION PER SERVE Protein 8 g; **Fat 1 g**; Carbohydrate 35 g; Dietary Fibre 5.5 g; Cholesterol 1 mg; 795 kJ (190 Cal)

Lemon-scented Broth with Tortellini

1 lemon
½ cup (125 ml/4 fl oz) white wine
440 g (14 oz) can chicken consommé
⅓ cup (20 g/¾ oz) chopped fresh parsley
375 g (12 oz) fresh or dried veal- or chicken-filled
tortellini

PREPARATION TIME 10 minutes
TOTAL COOKING TIME 20 minutes
SERVES 4–6

1 Using a vegetable peeler, peel wide strips from the lemon. Remove the white pith with a small sharp knife and cut three of the wide pieces into fine strips. Set these aside for garnishing.

2 Place the wide lemon strips, white wine, consommé and 3 cups (750 ml/ 24 fl oz) water in a large deep pan. Cook for 10 minutes over low heat. Remove the lemon rind and bring to the boil.

3 Add half the parsley, the tortellini and a sprinkling of black pepper to the pan. Cook for 6–7 minutes or until the pasta is al dente. Garnish with the remaining parsley and the fine strips of lemon.

Storage
If you want, you can prepare the recipe up to the end of step 2 and then leave in the fridge for a day before adding the pasta.

NUTRITION PER SERVE Protein 6 g; **Fat 4 g**; Carbohydrate 9 g; Dietary Fibre 2 g; Cholesterol 14 mg; 483 kJ (115 cal)

Asian Chicken Noodle Soup

90 g (3 oz) fresh egg noodles
5 cups (1.25 litres) chicken stock
1 tablespoon mirin (see NOTE)
2 tablespoons soy sauce
3 cm (1 inch) piece fresh ginger, julienned
2 chicken breast fillets, finely sliced

2 bunches baby bok choy, stalks trimmed,
leaves separated
fresh coriander leaves, to garnish

PREPARATION TIME 10 minutes
TOTAL COOKING TIME 10 minutes
SERVES 4

1 Soak the noodles in boiling water for 1 minute, drain and set aside. In a large saucepan, heat the stock to simmering, add the mirin, soy sauce, ginger, chicken and noodles. Cook for 5 minutes, or until the chicken is tender and the noodles are warmed through. Skim the surface of the soup.

2 Add the bok choy and cook for a further 2 minutes, or until the bok choy has wilted. Serve in deep Chinese bowls and garnish with fresh coriander leaves. Serve with sweet chilli sauce.

Note
Mirin is a Chinese sweet rice wine used for cooking. Sweet sherry, with a little sugar added, can be used if mirin is unavailable.

NUTRITION PER SERVE Protein 30 g; **Fat 3 g**; Carbohydrate 15 g; Dietary Fibre 1 g; Cholesterol 65 mg; 915 kJ (220 cal)

Pea and Ham Soup

500 g (1 lb) green split peas
1 kg (2 lb) ham hock or bacon bones, chopped
into short pieces
(ask your butcher to do this)
1 large onion, chopped
1 large carrot, chopped
1 celery stick, chopped

1 turnip, peeled and chopped
1 parsnip, peeled and chopped
3 tablespoons chopped fresh parsley

PREPARATION TIME 20 minutes + soaking
TOTAL COOKING TIME 1 hour 40 minutes
SERVES 10

1 Leave the peas for at least 4 hours in a large bowl of water. Drain, discarding the soaking water.

2 Put the hock or bones in a large heavy-based pan and add 2 litres water, the peas, onion, carrot, celery, turnip and parsnip. Bring slowly to the boil and then reduce the heat, cover partially and simmer for 1½ hours, or until the peas are reduced to a mush. Stir occasionally and skim the surface regularly to remove any froth, using either a spoon or a folded piece of paper towel. Remove the pan from the heat and allow to cool a little.

3 Lift out the hock or bones with a pair of tongs or a slotted spoon. Leave them to cool a little before removing the meat. Discard the bones, dice the meat and set aside.

4 When the soup has cooled, purée it in small batches in a food processor or blender. Return the soup to the pan and add the diced meat. Stir in the parsley and reheat gently to serve.

Storage
Refrigerate for up to 4 days or freeze for up to 1 month.

Hint
Ham hock has more meat than bacon bones, however bacon bones have a more intense flavour.

NUTRITION PER SERVE Protein 12 g; **Fat 1 g**; Carbohydrate 26 g; Dietary Fibre 6.5 g; Cholesterol 0 mg; 685 kJ (164 cal)

Vegetable Curry

2 teaspoons olive oil
1 onion, chopped
2 cloves garlic, crushed
2 teaspoons ground cumin
2 teaspoons ground coriander
3 teaspoons Madras curry powder
500 g (1 lb) potatoes, cut into bite-sized pieces
500 g (1 lb) pumpkin, cut into bite-sized pieces
2 large zucchini, thickly sliced
2 large carrots, thickly sliced

400 g (13 oz) can chopped tomatoes
1 cup (250 ml/8 fl oz) vegetable stock
100 g (3$\frac{1}{2}$ oz) broccoli florets
150 g (5 oz) green beans, cut into short lengths
$\frac{1}{4}$ cup (15 g/$\frac{1}{2}$ oz) chopped fresh coriander
1 cup (250 g/8 oz) low-fat natural yoghurt

PREPARATION TIME 30 minutes
TOTAL COOKING TIME 45 minutes
SERVES 6

1   Heat the oil in a large deep pan, add the onion and garlic and cook until softened. Add the ground cumin, coriander and curry powder and cook for 1–2 minutes, or until fragrant. Add the potato, pumpkin, zucchini and carrot and toss to coat in the spices.

2   Stir in the tomato and stock, bring to the boil, then reduce the heat and simmer, covered, for 30 minutes, or until the vegetables are tender, stirring frequently. Add the broccoli florets and chopped beans and simmer, uncovered, for 5 minutes, or until all the vegetables are tender. Stir in the chopped coriander and serve with yoghurt. Can be served with steamed rice.

NUTRITION PER SERVE Protein 8.5 g; **Fat 4 g**; Carbohydrate 25 g; Dietary Fibre 6 g; Cholesterol 7 mg; 715 kJ (170 cal)

Dry Potato and Pea Curry

750 g (1 ½ lb) potatoes, peeled
2 teaspoons brown mustard seeds
2 tablespoons ghee or oil
2 cloves garlic, crushed
2 teaspoons grated fresh ginger
2 onions, sliced
1 teaspoon turmeric
½ teaspoon chilli powder

1 teaspoon ground cumin
1 teaspoon garam masala
⅔ cup (100 g) fresh or frozen peas
2 tablespoons chopped fresh mint

PREPARATION TIME 15 minutes
TOTAL COOKING TIME 35 minutes
SERVES 4

1 Cut the potatoes into small cubes. Heat the mustard seeds in a dry pan until they start to pop. Add the ghee, garlic, ginger and onion to the pan and cook until soft. Add the potato, turmeric, chilli and cumin and season with salt and pepper.

2 Stir until the potatoes are coated with the spices. Add ½ cup (125 ml) of water to the pan, bring to the boil, reduce the heat and simmer, covered, for 15–20 minutes, or until tender, stirring occasionally.

3 Stir in the garam masala and peas. Simmer, covered, for 3–5 minutes, or until the potato is cooked and the liquid absorbed. Stir in the mint. Serve with Indian bread, such as naan.

NUTRITION PER SERVE Protein 7 g; **Fat 3 g**; Carbohydrate 3 g; Dietary Fibre 6 g; Cholesterol 0 mg; 725 kJ (175 cal)

Potato Gnocchi with Tomato Sauce

500 g (1 lb) floury potatoes, unpeeled
1 egg yolk
3 tablespoons grated Parmesan
1 cup (125 g/4 oz) plain flour

Tomato sauce
425 g (14 oz) can tomatoes
1 small onion, chopped
1 celery stick, chopped

1 small carrot, chopped
1 tablespoon shredded fresh basil
1 teaspoon chopped fresh thyme
1 clove garlic, crushed
1 teaspoon caster sugar

PREPARATION TIME 1 hour
TOTAL COOKING TIME 45 minutes
SERVES 4

1 Steam or boil the potatoes until just tender. Drain thoroughly and allow to cool for 10 minutes before peeling and mashing them.

2 Measure 2 cups of the mashed potato into a large bowl, mix in the egg yolk, Parmesan, 1/4 teaspoon of salt and some black pepper. Slowly add flour until you have a slightly sticky dough. Knead for 5 minutes, adding more flour if necessary, until a smooth dough is formed.

3 Divide the dough into four portions and roll each portion on a lightly floured surface to form a sausage shape, about 2 cm (3/4 inch) thick.

4 Cut the rolls into 2.5 cm (1 inch) slices and shape each piece into an oval. Press each oval into the palm of your hand against a floured fork, to flatten slightly and indent one side with a pattern. As you make the gnocchi place them in a single layer on a baking tray and cover until ready to use.

5 To make the tomato sauce, mix all the ingredients with salt and pepper in a pan. Bring to the boil, reduce the heat to medium-low and simmer for 30 minutes, stirring occasionally. Allow to cool, then process in a food processor or blender, until smooth. Reheat if necessary before serving.

6 Cook the gnocchi in batches in a large pan of boiling salted water for 2 minutes, or until the gnocchi float to the surface. Drain well. Serve the gnocchi tossed through the sauce.

Notes
The gnocchi can be prepared several hours in advance and arranged on a tray in a single layer to prevent them sticking together. Cover and keep refrigerated.

Gnocchi was traditionally made using potatoes baked in their skins. This results in a drier dough that is easy to work with, so if you have time you can use this method.

NUTRITION PER SERVE Protein 10 g; **Fat 4 g**; Carbohydrate 45 g; Dietary Fibre 5 g; Cholesterol 50 mg; 1125 kJ (270 cal)

Pasta with Roasted Tomato Sauce

1 kg (2 lb) ripe Roma tomatoes
8 cloves garlic, unpeeled
2 tablespoons olive oil
2 teaspoons dried basil
1 cup (250 ml/8 fl oz) vegetable stock
$\frac{1}{2}$ cup (125 m$\frac{1}{4}$ fl oz) dry white wine
2 tablespoons balsamic vinegar

500 g (1 lb) tagliatelle
2 tablespoons grated Parmesan

PREPARATION TIME 25 minutes
TOTAL COOKING TIME 50 minutes
SERVES 4

1 Preheat the oven to moderate 180°C (350°F/Gas 4). Cut the tomatoes in half lengthways and arrange, cut-side-up, in the base of a baking dish. Sprinkle with 1 tablespoon water to prevent the tomatoes catching. Add the garlic to the pan and drizzle or brush the oil over the tomatoes and garlic. Sprinkle with basil, salt and freshly ground black pepper. Bake for 25 minutes, or until soft, and gently remove from the pan.

2 Heat the baking dish over low heat and add the stock, white wine and vinegar. Bring to the boil, reduce the heat and simmer for 20 minutes. Roughly chop the tomatoes, retaining all the juices. Squeeze the garlic out of the skin and add the tomato and garlic to the simmering sauce. Taste and adjust the seasonings.

3 Cook the pasta in a large pan of rapidly boiling salted water for about 10 minutes, or until al dente. Drain and keep warm. Serve the sauce over the pasta and sprinkle with Parmesan.

NUTRITION PER SERVE Protein 20 g; **Fat 3.5 g**; Carbohydrate 95 g; Dietary Fibre 10 g; Cholesterol 5 mg; 2060 kJ (515 cal)

Steamed Seafood Rolls

Soy and ginger sauce
¼ cup (60 ml) light soy sauce
2 teaspoons finely chopped fresh ginger
2 cloves garlic, finely crushed
1 teaspoon sugar

6 Chinese broccoli leaves, finely shredded
4 fresh rice noodle rolls
24 raw prawns, peeled and deveined
3 cloves garlic, crushed
3 teaspoons finely chopped fresh ginger
5 spring onions, finely sliced

PREPARATION TIME 40 minutes
TOTAL COOKING TIME 20 minutes
SERVES 4–6

1 To make the soy and ginger sauce, combine all the ingredients, mix well and set aside.

2 Steam the Chinese broccoli leaves until just wilted.

3 Carefully unroll a rice noodle roll and cut it in half. Place 3 prawns and a little garlic and ginger on the cut end of each half, but not all the way to the end. Top with some spring onion and Chinese broccoli. Fold both sides of the noodle in towards the centre, then roll up the noodle like a spring roll. Cover with a slightly damp tea towel while preparing the rest of the rolls.

4 Place 3–4 rolls in a large bamboo steamer lined with baking paper. Place over a wok or pan of boiling water and steam for 7–10 minutes, or until the prawns are cooked. Remove the rolls, cover with foil and keep warm while cooking the remainder. Serve with the soy and ginger sauce.

NUTRITION PER SERVE (6): Protein 20 g; **Fat 1 g**; Carbohydrate 6 g; Dietary Fibre 3 g; Cholesterol 115 mg; 450 kJ (105 cal)

Prawn Fried Rice

4 egg whites, lightly beaten
cooking oil spray
2 cloves garlic, crushed
350 g (12 oz) raw prawns, peeled, deveined and
halved lengthways
100 g (3½ oz) cooked chicken, shredded
½ cup (80 g/2¾ oz) frozen peas
180 g (6 oz) sliced light ham, cut into small strips
1 red capsicum, diced
4 spring onions, sliced

4 cups (750 g/1½ lb) cooked white and
wild rice blend
1½ tablespoons soy sauce
3 teaspoons fish sauce
1½ teaspoons soft brown sugar

PREPARATION TIME 20 minutes
TOTAL COOKING TIME 15 minutes
SERVES 6

1 Lightly spray a non-stick wok with oil and pour in the egg white. Cook over low heat, stirring until the egg is just cooked and slightly scrambled, then remove and set aside.

2 Add the garlic, prawns, chicken, peas, ham and capsicum to the wok and stir-fry for 3–4 minutes, or until the prawns are cooked.

3 Add the spring onion, rice, soy and fish sauces and sugar and toss for 30 seconds, or until heated through. Add the egg, toss lightly and serve.

Hint
You will need to cook 1⅓ cups (260 g/8 oz) rice for this recipe.

NUTRITION PER SERVE Protein 35 g; **Fat 3 g**; Carbohydrate 105 g; Dietary Fibre 4 g; Cholesterol 120 mg; 2500 kJ (600 cal)

Thai-style Whole Snapper

2 garlic cloves, crushed
1 tablespoon fish sauce
2 tablespoons lemon juice
1 tablespoon grated fresh ginger
2 tablespoons sweet chilli sauce
1 tablespoon rice wine vinegar
2 tablespoons chopped fresh coriander
2 tablespoons white wine

600 g (1 1/4 lb) whole snapper, cleaned and
scaled (ask your fishmonger to do this)
2 spring onions, cut into thin strips

PREPARATION TIME 10 minutes
TOTAL COOKING TIME 30 minutes
SERVES 6

1 Preheat the oven to moderately hot 190°C (375°F/
Gas 5). Place the crushed garlic, fish sauce, lemon
juice, grated ginger, sweet chilli sauce, rice wine
vinegar, coriander and wine in a small jug and mix
together well.

2 Place the snapper on a large piece of foil on a
baking tray. Pour the marinade over the fish and
sprinkle with the spring onion.

3 Wrap some foil around the fish like a parcel and
place in the oven. Bake for 20–30 minutes or until
the flesh flakes easily when tested with a fork.
Serve immediately with steamed rice.

NUTRITION PER SERVE Protein 20 g; **Fat 2 g**; Carbohydrate 5 g; Dietary Fibre 0 g; Cholesterol 60 mg; 495 kJ (120 Cal)

Chargrilled Chicken

4 chicken breast fillets
2 tablespoons honey
1 tablespoon wholegrain mustard
1 tablespoon soy sauce
2 red onions, cut into wedges
8 Roma tomatoes, halved lengthways
2 tablespoons soft brown sugar
2 tablespoons balsamic vinegar

cooking oil spray
snow pea sprouts, for serving

PREPARATION TIME 20 minutes + 2 hours refrigeration
TOTAL COOKING TIME 50 minutes
SERVES 4

1 Preheat the oven to moderate 180°C (350°F/Gas 4). Trim the chicken of any fat and place in a shallow dish. Combine the honey, mustard and soy sauce and pour over the chicken, tossing to coat. Cover and refrigerate for 2 hours, turning once.

2 Place the onion wedges and tomato halves on a baking tray covered with baking paper. Sprinkle with the sugar and drizzle with the balsamic vinegar. Bake for 40 minutes.

3 Heat a chargrill pan and lightly spray with oil. Remove the chicken from the marinade and cook for 4–5 minutes on each side, or until cooked through. Slice and serve with the snow pea sprouts, tomato halves and onion wedges.

NUTRITION PER SERVE Protein 25 g; **Fat 2.5 g**; Carbohydrate 30 g; Dietary Fibre 3 g; Cholesterol 50 mg; 990 kJ (235 cal)

Sweet Chilli Chicken

1 kg (2 lb) chicken thigh fillets
2 tablespoons lime juice
½ cup (125 ml/4 fl oz) sweet chilli sauce
3 tablespoons kecap manis
(see NOTE)

PREPARATION TIME 15 minutes +
2 hours refrigeration
TOTAL COOKING TIME 20 minutes
SERVES 6

1 Trim any excess fat from the chicken thigh fillets and cut them in half. Put the chicken in a shallow non-metallic dish.

2 Place the lime juice, sweet chilli sauce and kecap manis in a bowl and whisk to combine.

3 Pour the marinade over the chicken, cover and refrigerate for 2 hours.

4 Chargrill or bake in a preheated moderately hot 200°C (400°F/Gas 6) oven for 20 minutes, or until the chicken is tender and cooked through and the marinade has caramelised.

Note
Kecap manis (ketjap manis) is a thick Indonesian sauce, similar to—but sweeter than—soy sauce, and is generally flavoured with garlic and star anise. Store in a cool, dry place and refrigerate after opening. If not available, use soy sauce sweetened with a little soft brown sugar.

NUTRITION PER SERVE Protein 35 g; **Fat 4.5 g**; Carbohydrate 4 g; Dietary Fibre 1 g; Cholesterol 85 mg; 880 kJ (210 cal)

Tandoori Chicken

½ cup (125 g/4 oz) Greek-style
low-fat natural yoghurt
2 tablespoons tandoori paste
2 cloves garlic, crushed
2 tablespoons lime juice
1½ teaspoons garam masala
2 tablespoons finely chopped fresh coriander
leaves
6 chicken thigh fillets, fat removed

PREPARATION TIME 10 minutes +
1 hour marinating
TOTAL COOKING TIME 15 minutes
SERVES 4

1 Combine the yoghurt, tandoori paste, garlic, lime juice, garam masala and coriander in a bowl and mix well.

2 Add the chicken, coat well, cover and refrigerate for at least 1 hour.

3 Preheat a barbecue or chargrill plate and lightly brush with oil. Cook the chicken, in batches if necessary, for 10–15 minutes on medium heat, turning once and basting with the remaining marinade until golden and cooked through. Serve with cucumber raita and naan bread.

NUTRITION PER SERVE Protein 27 g; **Fat 3.5 g**; Carbohydrate 2 g; Dietary Fibre 0 g; Cholesterol 60 mg; 635 kJ (150 cal)

Chicken with Corn Salsa

Corn salsa
2 corn cobs
olive oil, for brushing
500 g (1 lb) pawpaw, peeled, seeded and cut
into cubes
2 tomatoes, finely chopped
3 spring onions, finely chopped
3 tablespoons chopped fresh mint

1 small red chilli, seeded and chopped
2 tablespoons lemon juice
4 chicken breast fillets

PREPARATION TIME 30 minutes
TOTAL COOKING TIME 25 minutes
SERVES 4

1 To make the salsa, heat a chargrill pan or barbecue grill or flatplate. Lightly brush the corn with olive oil and cook, turning frequently, for about 10 minutes, or until lightly browned all over. Brush with some oil while cooking. Cool, then strip the corn of its kernels using a sharp knife. Combine the corn, pawpaw, tomato, spring onion, mint, red chilli and lemon juice in a bowl.

2 Remove any excess fat or sinew from the chicken. Brush the fillets with some oil and cook for 4–6 minutes each side, or until tender. Serve with the corn salsa.

NUTRITION PER SERVE Protein 20 g; **Fat 4 g**; Carbohydrate 25 g; Dietary Fibre 5 g; Cholesterol 55 mg; 950 kJ (225 cal)

Chicken with Baked Eggplant and Tomato

1 red capsicum
1 eggplant
3 tomatoes, cut into quarters
200 g (6½ oz) large button mushrooms, halved
1 onion, cut into thin wedges
cooking oil spray
1½ tablespoons tomato paste
½ cup (125 ml/4 fl oz) chicken stock

¼ cup (60 ml/2 fl oz) white wine
2 lean bacon rashers, rind removed
4 chicken breast fillets
4 small sprigs fresh rosemary

PREPARATION TIME 30 minutes
TOTAL COOKING TIME 1½ hours
SERVES 4

1 Preheat the oven to moderately hot 200°C (400°F/Gas 6). Cut the capsicum and eggplant into bite-sized pieces and combine with the tomato, mushrooms and onion in a baking dish. Spray with oil and bake for 1 hour, or until starting to brown and soften, stirring once.

2 Pour the combined tomato paste, stock and wine into the dish and bake for 10 minutes, or until thickened.

3 Meanwhile, cut the bacon in half. Wrap a strip around each chicken breast and secure it underneath with a toothpick. Poke a sprig of fresh rosemary underneath the bacon. Pan-fry in a lightly oiled, non-stick frying pan, over medium heat, until golden on both sides. Cover and cook for 10–15 minutes, or until the chicken is cooked through. Remove the toothpicks. Serve the chicken on the vegetables, surrounded with sauce.

NUTRITION PER SERVE Protein 35 g; **Fat 4.5 g**; Carbohydrate 8 g; Dietary Fibre 5 g; Cholesterol 70 mg; 965 kJ (230 cal)

Sweet and Sour Pork Kebabs

1 kg (2 lb) lean pork fillets
1 large red capsicum
1 large green capsicum
425 g (14 oz) can pineapple pieces
1 cup (250 ml) orange juice
¼ cup (60 ml) white vinegar
2 tablespoons soft brown sugar

2 teaspoons chilli garlic sauce
2 teaspoons cornflour

PREPARATION TIME 30 minutes + 3 hours marinating
TOTAL COOKING TIME 20 minutes
SERVES 6

1 Trim the pork of excess fat and sinew, then cut into 2.5 cm (1 inch) cubes. Cut both the capsicums into 2 cm (¾ inch) squares. Drain the pineapple and reserve the juice. Thread the meat, alternately with the capsicum and pineapple, onto skewers. Combine the reserved pineapple juice with the orange juice, vinegar, sugar and sauce. Place the kebabs in a shallow non-metal dish and pour half the juice mixture over the top. Refrigerate, covered with plastic wrap, for several hours or overnight, turning occasionally. Prepare and heat a barbecue 1 hour before cooking.

2 Place the remaining marinade in a small saucepan. Combine the cornflour with 1 tablespoon of the marinade, then add to the pan. Stir over medium heat until the mixture boils and thickens, then transfer to a small serving bowl. Cover with plastic wrap and leave to cool.

3 Cook the kebabs on a hot lightly oiled barbecue grill or flatplate for 15 minutes, or until tender, turning occasionally. Serve with the sweet and sour sauce.

NUTRITION PER SERVE Protein 31.5 g; **Fat 2.5 g**; Carbohydrate 19.5 g; Dietary Fibre 1 g; Cholesterol 65.5 mg; 950 kJ (225 cal)

Pork, Bok Choy and Black Bean Stir-fry

400 g (13 oz) lean pork leg steaks
1 tablespoon canned salted black beans, rinsed
500 g (1 lb) baby bok choy
2 teaspoons sesame oil
2 onions, finely sliced
2 cloves garlic, finely chopped
2–3 teaspoons chopped ginger
1 red capsicum, cut into strips

½ cup (90 g/3 oz) water chestnuts, finely sliced
2 tablespoons oyster sauce
1 tablespoon soy sauce
2 teaspoons fish sauce

PREPARATION TIME 20 minutes
TOTAL COOKING TIME 10 minutes
SERVES 4

1 Slice the pork steaks into strips, cutting across the grain. Roughly chop the beans. Cut the ends off the bok choy, separate the leaves and shred.

2 Heat half the sesame oil in a large non-stick frying pan or wok. Cook the onion, garlic and ginger over high heat for 3–4 minutes, add the capsicum and cook for 2–3 minutes. Remove from the pan. Heat the remaining sesame oil and stir-fry the pork in batches over high heat.

3 Return all the pork to the pan along with the onion mixture, black beans, shredded bok choy, water chestnuts and oyster, soy and fish sauces. Toss quickly to combine the ingredients, lower the heat and cover and steam for 3–4 minutes, or until the bok choy has just wilted. Serve immediately.

NUTRITION PER SERVE Protein 30 g; **Fat 3 g**; Carbohydrate 20 g; Dietary Fibre 3.5 g; Cholesterol 55 mg; 910 kJ (215 cal)

Spicy Grilled Pork

2 tablespoons kecap manis
2 teaspoons grated fresh ginger
2 teaspoons sambal oelek
1 tablespoon soft brown sugar
1 clove garlic, crushed
4 butterflied pork steaks
1 lemon, cut into wedges

Salad
200 g (6½ oz) mixed lettuce leaves
1 Lebanese cucumber, thinly sliced
1 Granny Smith apple, cut into thick matchsticks

PREPARATION TIME 15 minutes
TOTAL COOKING TIME 10 minutes
SERVES 4

1 Combine the kecap manis, ginger, sambal oelek, sugar and garlic a bowl. Add the pork and cover with the marinade.

2 To make the salad, combine the lettuce, cucumber and apple and toss together in a large bowl.

3 Place the pork steaks under a hot grill and cook for 4 minutes on each side, or until the meat is cooked through. Baste with the remaining marinade while cooking. Serve with the salad and lemon wedges.

NUTRITION PER SERVE Protein 25 g; **Fat 2 g**; Carbohydrate 8.5 g; Dietary Fibre 2.5 g; Cholesterol 55 mg; 655 kJ (155 cal)

Rosemary Beef Skewers

350 g (11$\frac{1}{2}$ oz) rump steak
12 long sprigs rosemary
12 (60 g–2 oz) Swiss brown mushrooms, halved
1 tablespoon oil
1 tablespoon honey
1 tablespoon soy sauce

PREPARATION TIME 15 minutes
TOTAL COOKING TIME 10 minutes
SERVES 4

1 Trim the meat of any excess fat and sinew and cut into 2.5 cm (1 inch) cubes. Trim the leaves from the stems of the rosemary sprigs, leaving 5 cm (2 inches) at one end. Thread the meat alternately with the mushrooms onto the rosemary skewers. Place the oil, honey and soy sauce in a small bowl and mix together well.

2 Place the skewers on a lightly oiled grill tray and brush the meat with the oil and honey mixture. Cook under a hot grill for 10 minutes, or until tender, turning occasionally and brushing with the oil and honey mixture. Serve immediately with a green salad.

NUTRITION PER SERVE Protein 20 g; **Fat 2.5 g**; Carbohydrate 6 g; Dietary Fibre 0.5 g; Cholesterol 60 mg; 545 kJ (130 cal)

Beef and Vegetable Casserole

500 g (1 lb) lean round steak
cooking oil spray
1 onion, sliced
3 cloves garlic, crushed
2 teaspoons ground cumin
1 teaspoon dried thyme leaves
2 bay leaves
400 g (13 oz) can chopped tomatoes
500 g (1 lb) potatoes, chopped
2 large carrots, thickly sliced

4 zucchini, thickly sliced
250 g (8 oz) mushrooms, halved
250 g (8 oz) yellow squash, halved
2 tablespoons tomato paste
$1/2$ cup (125 ml/4 fl oz) red wine
$1/3$ cup (20 g/$3/4$ oz) chopped fresh parsley

PREPARATION TIME 40 minutes
TOTAL COOKING TIME 1 hour 40 minutes
SERVES 6

1 Preheat the oven to moderate 180°C (350°F/Gas 4). Remove any excess fat and sinew from the meat and cut into 2 cm ($3/4$ inch) cubes. Spray a deep, non-stick frying pan with oil and fry the meat in batches until brown. Remove from the pan. Spray the pan again, add the onion and cook until lightly golden. Add the garlic, cumin, thyme and bay leaves; stir for 1 minute.

2 Return the meat and any juices to the pan, tossing to coat with spices. Add $1\frac{1}{2}$ cups (375 ml/12 fl oz) water and the tomato, scraping the pan. Simmer for 10 minutes, or until thickened. Mix in a large casserole dish with the vegetables, tomato paste and wine.

3 Bake, covered, for 1 hour. Stir well, then uncover and bake for 20 minutes. Season, remove the bay leaves and stir in the parsley.

NUTRITION PER SERVE Protein 25 g; **Fat 4 g**; Carbohydrate 20 g; Dietary Fibre 6.5 g; Cholesterol 50 mg; 930 kJ (220 cal)

Beef Stroganoff

500 g (1 lb) rump steak
cooking oil spray
1 onion, sliced
¼ teaspoon paprika
250 g (8 oz) button mushrooms, halved
2 tablespoons tomato paste
½ cup (125 ml/4 fl oz) beef stock

½ cup (125 ml) low-fat light evaporated milk
3 teaspoons cornflour
chopped fresh parsley, for serving

PREPARATION TIME 20 minutes
TOTAL COOKING TIME 25 minutes
SERVES 4

1 Remove any excess fat from the steak and slice into thin strips. Cook in batches in a large, lightly greased non-stick frying pan over high heat, until just cooked. Remove from the pan.

2 Lightly spray the pan and cook the onion, paprika and mushrooms over medium heat until the onion has softened. Add the meat, tomato paste, stock and ½ cup (125 ml) water. Bring to the boil, then reduce the heat and simmer for 10 minutes.

3 In a small bowl, mix the evaporated milk with the cornflour. Add to the pan and stir until the sauce boils and thickens. Season well and sprinkle with parsley. Delicious over pasta.

NUTRITION PER SERVE Protein 35 g; **Fat 4 g**; Carbohydrate 8 g; Dietary Fibre 2.5 g; Cholesterol 85 mg; 900 kJ (215 cal)

Fudge Brownies

cooking oil spray
1/2 cup (60 g/2 oz) plain flour
1/2 cup (60 g/2 oz) self-raising flour
1 teaspoon bicarbonate of soda
3/4 cup (90 g/3 oz) cocoa powder
2 eggs
1 1/4 cups (310 g/10 oz) caster sugar
2 teaspoons vanilla essence

2 tablespoons vegetable oil
200 g (6 1/2 oz) low-fat fromage frais
140 ml (4 1/2 fl oz) apple purée
icing sugar, for dusting

PREPARATION TIME 15 minutes
TOTAL COOKING TIME 30 minutes
MAKES 18 pieces

1 Preheat the oven to moderate 180°C (350°F/Gas 4). Spray a 30 x 20 cm (12 x 8 inch) shallow baking tin with oil and line the base of the tin with baking paper.

2 Sift the flours, bicarbonate of soda and cocoa powder into a large bowl. Mix the eggs, sugar, vanilla essence, oil, fromage frais and purée in a large bowl, stirring until well combined. Add to the flour and stir until combined. Spread into the prepared tin and bake for about 30 minutes, or until a skewer inserted in the centre comes out clean.

3 The brownie will sink slightly in the centre as it cools. Leave in the pan for 5 minutes before turning onto a wire rack to cool. Dust with icing sugar before cutting into pieces to serve.

NUTRITION PER PIECE Protein 2.5 g; **Fat 3.5 g**; Carbohydrate 2.5 g; Dietary Fibre 5 g; Cholesterol 20 mg; 595 kJ (140 cal)

Mango and Passionfruit Sorbet

1 cup (250 g/8 oz) caster sugar
$^1/_3$ cup (90 g/3 oz) passionfruit pulp
$^1/_2$ large mango (200 g/6$^1/_2$ oz), chopped
1 large (250 g/8 oz) peach, chopped
2 tablespoons lemon juice
1 egg white

PREPARATION TIME 20 minutes + 8 hours freezing
TOTAL COOKING TIME 5 minutes
SERVES 6

1 Stir the sugar in a pan with 1 cup (250 ml/8 fl oz) water over low heat until dissolved. Increase the heat, bring to the boil and boil for 1 minute. Transfer to a glass bowl, cool, then refrigerate. Strain the passionfruit pulp, reserving 1 tablespoon of the seeds.

2 Blend the fruit, passionfruit juice and lemon juice in a blender until smooth. With the motor running, add the cold sugar syrup and 150 ml (5 fl oz) water. Stir in the passionfruit seeds. Freeze in a shallow container, stirring occasionally, for about 5 hours, or until almost set.

3 Break up the icy mixture roughly with a fork or spoon, transfer to a bowl and beat with electric beaters until smooth and fluffy. Beat the egg white in a small bowl until firm peaks form, then fold into the mixture until just combined. Spread into a loaf tin and return to the freezer until firm. Transfer to the refrigerator, to soften, 15 minutes before serving.

Variation

To make a berry sorbet, use 200 g (6$^1/_2$ oz) blackberries or blueberries, 200 g (6$^1/_2$ oz) hulled strawberries and 50 g (1$^3/_4$ oz) peach flesh. Prepare as above.

NUTRITION PER SERVE Protein 2 g; **Fat 0 g**; Carbohydrate 50 g; Dietary Fibre 3 g; Cholesterol 0 mg; 850 kJ (200 cal)

Berries in Champagne Jelly

1 litre champagne or sparkling wine
1¹⁄₂ tablespoons gelatine
1 cup (250 g/8 oz) sugar
4 strips lemon rind
4 strips orange rind

1²⁄₃ cups (250 g/8 oz) small strawberries, hulled
1²⁄₃ cups (250 g/8 oz) blueberries

PREPARATION TIME 10 minutes + refrigeration
TOTAL COOKING TIME 5 minutes
SERVES 8

1 Pour 2 cups (500 ml/16 fl oz) champagne or sparkling white wine into a bowl and let the bubbles subside. Sprinkle the gelatine over the top in an even layer. Leave until the gelatine is spongy—do not stir. Place the remaining champagne in a large pan with the sugar, lemon and orange rind and heat gently, stirring, until all the sugar has dissolved.

2 Remove the pan from the heat, add the gelatine mixture and stir until thoroughly dissolved. Leave the jelly to cool completely, then remove the lemon and orange rind.

3 Divide the strawberries and blueberries among eight ¹⁄₂ cup (125 ml/4 fl oz) glasses or bowls and pour the jelly over them. Chill until the jelly has fully set. Remove from the fridge 15 minutes before serving.

NUTRITION PER SERVE Protein 3 g; **Fat 0 g**; Carbohydrate 37 g; Dietary Fibre 1.5 g; Cholesterol 0 mg; 965 kJ (230 cal)

Raspberry Mousse

3 teaspoons gelatine
1 cup (250 g/8 oz) low-fat vanilla yoghurt
2 x 200 g (6½ oz) tubs low-fat fromage frais or
light vanilla Fruche
4 egg whites

150 g (5 oz) raspberries, mashed
fresh raspberries and mint leaves, for serving

PREPARATION TIME 30 minutes + refrigeration
TOTAL COOKING TIME Nil
SERVES 4

1 Sprinkle the gelatine in an even layer onto
1 tablespoon water in a small bowl and leave to
go spongy. Bring a small pan of water to the boil,
remove from the heat and place the bowl in the
pan. Stir until clear.

2 In a large bowl, stir the vanilla yoghurt and
fromage frais together, then add the gelatine and
mix well.

3 Using electric beaters, beat the egg whites until
stiff peaks form, then fold through the yoghurt
mixture. Transfer half to a separate bowl and fold
the mashed raspberries through.

4 Divide the raspberry mixture into the bases of
4 long glasses or serving bowls. Top with the
vanilla mixture. Refrigerate for several hours, or
until set. Decorate with fresh raspberries and
mint leaves.

NUTRITION PER SERVE Protein 9.5 g; **Fat 2 g**; Carbohydrate 10 g; Dietary Fibre 2 g; Cholesterol 4 mg; 355 kJ (85 cal)

Lime Delicious

60 g (2 oz) light cream cheese, softened
½ cup (125 g/4 oz) caster sugar
2 tablespoons self-raising flour
½ teaspoon finely grated lime rind
¼ cup (60 ml/2 fl oz) lime juice
200 ml (6½ fl oz) skim milk
2 egg whites

icing sugar, to dust
lime slices, to garnish

PREPARATION TIME 20 minutes
TOTAL COOKING TIME 30 minutes
SERVES 4

1 Preheat the oven to moderate 180°C (350°F/ Gas 4). Combine the cream cheese and sugar in a large bowl. Stir in the flour and lime rind, then gradually stir in the lime juice and the milk, until just smooth. Do not overmix.

2 Beat the egg whites with electric beaters in a clean, dry bowl until soft peaks form. Using a large metal spoon, gently fold the egg whites into the lime mixture. Spoon into four 1 cup (250 ml/8 fl oz) ovenproof dishes.

3 Place the dishes in a large roasting tin. Pour in enough hot water to come halfway up the sides of the dishes and bake for 30 minutes, or until set in the centre. Dust with icing sugar, garnish with a slice of lime, and serve hot.

Note
Make sure you just combine the cream cheese with the sugar, rather than beat until smooth. If beaten, the cream cheese becomes grainy and can curdle when baked.

NUTRITION PER SERVE: Protein 6 g; **Fat 3 g**; Carbohydrate 31 g; Dietary Fibre 0.5 g; Cholesterol 9 mg; 700 kJ (165 Cal)

Pears Poached in Dark Grape Juice

6 beurre bosc (or any firm) pears
2 tablespoons lemon juice
2 cups (500 ml/8 fl oz) dark grape juice
2 cups (500 ml/8 fl oz) blackcurrant juice
2 tablespoons sweet sherry
4 cloves
350 g (11 oz) black grapes
1 cup (250 g/8 oz) low-fat natural yoghurt

1/2 teaspoon ground cinnamon
1 tablespoon honey

PREPARATION TIME 15 minutes + overnight refrigeration
TOTAL COOKING TIME 1 hour 20 minutes
SERVES 6

1 Core and peel the pears, leaving the stalks on. Place the pears, as you peel, in a bowl filled with cold water and the lemon juice, to prevent browning.

2 Put the grape and blackcurrant juices, sherry and cloves in a saucepan large enough to hold the pears. (The size of the saucepan will depend on the size of the pears.) Add the pears.

3 Bring the liquid to the boil, then reduce to a simmer. Cover and cook for 35–40 minutes, or until tender. Remove from the heat and leave the pears to cool in the syrup. Transfer the pears and syrup to a bowl and cover with plastic wrap. Refrigerate overnight.

4 To serve, strain the syrup into a pan, bring to the boil, then reduce to a simmer and cook for 40 minutes, or until reduced by about two-thirds. Cool slightly, place a pear on each plate and pour syrup over the pears. Arrange the grapes next to the pears. Just before serving, mix the yoghurt, cinnamon and honey and spoon over the pears or serve on the side.

NUTRITION PER SERVE Protein 4 g; **Fat 0 g**; Carbohydrate 95 g; Dietary Fibre 4 g; Cholesterol 2 mg; 1630 kJ (390 cal)

Chocolate Self-saucing Puddings

2 tablespoons cocoa powder
1 cup (125 g/4 oz) self-raising flour
60 g (2 oz) light cream cheese
1 teaspoon finely grated orange rind
$\frac{1}{2}$ cup (125 g/4 oz) caster sugar
$\frac{1}{2}$ cup (125 ml/4 fl oz) skim milk
$\frac{1}{3}$ cup (80 ml/ $2\frac{3}{4}$ fl oz) freshly squeezed
orange juice

$\frac{1}{2}$ cup (95 g/3 oz) soft brown sugar
1 tablespoon cocoa powder, extra
icing sugar, to dust

PREPARATION TIME 15 minutes
TOTAL COOKING TIME 35 minutes
SERVES 4

1 Preheat the oven to moderate 180°C (350°F/ Gas 4). Sift the cocoa powder with the flour, at least twice. Using a wooden spoon, blend the cream cheese, orange rind and sugar until smooth. Do not overmix.

2 Fold the milk and dry ingredients alternately into the cream cheese mixture, then stir in the orange juice. Pour the pudding mixture into four $1\frac{1}{2}$ cup (375 ml) ovenproof ramekins.

3 Combine the brown sugar and extra cocoa, and sprinkle evenly over the puddings. Carefully pour $\frac{1}{2}$ cup (125 ml) boiling water over each pudding and place on a baking tray. Bake the puddings for 35 minutes, or until firm. Serve dusted with icing sugar.

NUTRITION PER SERVE Protein 7 g; **Fat 3.5 g**; Carbohydrate 82 g; Dietary Fibre 1.5 g; Cholesterol 8.5 mg; 1575 kJ (375 Cal)

Tofu Salad with Ginger Miso Dressing

90 ml (3 fl oz) light soy sauce
2 teaspoons soy bean oil
2 cloves garlic, crushed
1 teaspoon grated fresh ginger
1 teaspoon chilli paste
500 g (1 lb) firm tofu, cut into small cubes
400 g (13 oz) mesclun leaves
1 Lebanese cucumber, finely sliced
250 g (8 oz) cherry tomatoes, halved
2 teaspoons soy bean oil, extra

Dressing
2 teaspoons white miso paste (see NOTE)
2 tablespoons mirin
1 teaspoon sesame oil
1 teaspoon grated fresh ginger
1 teaspoon finely chopped chives
1 tablespoon toasted sesame seeds

PREPARATION TIME 20 minutes +
overnight marinating
TOTAL COOKING TIME 5 minutes
SERVES 4

1 Mix together the tamari, soy bean oil, garlic, ginger, chilli paste and ½ teaspoon salt in a bowl. Add the tofu and mix until well coated. Marinate for at least 10 minutes, or preferably overnight. Drain and reserve the marinade.

2 To make the dressing, combine the miso with ½ cup (125 ml/4 fl oz) hot water and leave until the miso dissolves. Add the mirin, sesame oil, ginger, chives and sesame seeds and stir until beginning to thicken.

3 Put the mesclun leaves, cucumber and tomato in a serving bowl.

4 Heat the extra soy bean oil on a chargrill or hotplate. Add the tofu and cook over medium heat for 4 minutes, or until golden brown. Pour on the reserved marinade and cook for a further 1 minute over high heat. Remove from the grill and cool for 5 minutes.

5 Add the tofu to the salad, drizzle with the dressing and toss well.

Note

Miso is Japanese bean paste and is commonly used in soups, dressings, on grilled foods and as a flavouring for pickles.

NUTRITION PER SERVE Protein 12 g; **Fat 8 g**; Carbohydrate 4 g; Dietary Fibre 4 g; Cholesterol 0 mg; 590 kJ (140 cal)

Lime and Prawn Salad

200 g (6½ oz) baby green beans
2 Lebanese cucumbers, sliced
4 spring onions, finely chopped
1 tablespoon finely shredded kaffir lime leaves
¼ cup (15 g/½ oz) flaked coconut
750 g (1½ lb) cooked prawns, peeled, tails intact
2 teaspoons shredded lime rind

Dressing
1 tablespoon peanut oil
1 tablespoon nam pla (Thai fish sauce)
1 tablespoon grated palm sugar
1 tablespoon chopped fresh coriander
2 teaspoons soy sauce
1–2 teaspoons sweet chilli sauce
¼ cup (60 ml/2 fl oz) lime juice

PREPARATION TIME 35 minutes
TOTAL COOKING TIME 2 minutes
SERVES 4

1 Cook the beans in a small pan of boiling water for 2 minutes. Drain and cover with cold water, then drain again and pat dry with paper towels.

2 To make the dressing, whisk the ingredients in a bowl.

3 Combine the beans, cucumber, spring onion, lime leaves, flaked coconut and prawns in a large bowl. Add the dressing and toss gently to combine. Place the salad in a large serving bowl and garnish with the shredded lime rind.

Notes
Young lemon leaves can be used in place of the kaffir lime leaves if they are not available.

Soft brown or dark brown sugar may be substituted for the palm sugar.

NUTRITION PER SERVE Protein 45 g; **Fat 8 g**; Carbohydrate 7 g; Dietary Fibre 3 g; Cholesterol 350 mg; 1200 kJ (285 cal)

Chargrilled Tuna and Ruby Grapefruit Salad

4 ruby grapefruit
cooking oil spray
3 tuna steaks
150 g (5 oz) rocket leaves
1 red onion, sliced

Dressing
2 tablespoons almond oil
2 tablespoons raspberry vinegar
$1/2$ teaspoon sugar
1 tablespoon shredded fresh mint

PREPARATION TIME 20 minutes
TOTAL COOKING TIME 10 minutes
SERVES 6

1 Cut a slice off each end of the grapefruit and peel away the skin, removing all the pith. Separate the segments and set aside in a bowl.

2 Heat a chargrill plate and spray lightly with oil. Cook each tuna steak for 3–4 minutes on each side. This will leave the centre slightly pink. Cool, then thinly slice or flake.

3 To make the dressing, put the almond oil, vinegar, sugar and mint in a small screw-top jar and shake until well combined.

4 Place the rocket on a serving plate and top with the grapefruit segments, then the tuna and onion. Drizzle with the dressing and serve.

NUTRITION PER SERVE Protein 15 g; **Fat 7 g**; Carbohydrate 8 g; Dietary Fibre 2 g; Cholesterol 50 mg; 1015 kJ (240 cal)

Tandoori Lamb Salad

1 cup (250 g/8 oz) low-fat natural yoghurt
2 cloves garlic, crushed
2 teaspoons grated ginger
2 teaspoons ground turmeric
2 teaspoons garam masala
¼ teaspoon paprika
2 teaspoons ground coriander
red food colouring, optional
500 g (1 lb) lean lamb fillets
4 tablespoons lemon juice

1½ teaspoons chopped fresh coriander
1 teaspoon chopped fresh mint
150 g (5 oz) mixed salad leaves
1 large mango, cut into strips
2 cucumbers, cut into matchsticks

PREPARATION TIME 20 minutes + overnight marinating
TOTAL COOKING TIME 15 minutes
SERVES 4

1 Mix the yoghurt, garlic, ginger and spices in a bowl, add a little colouring and toss with the lamb to thoroughly coat. Cover and refrigerate overnight.

2 Grill the lamb on a foil-lined baking tray under high heat for 7 minutes each side, or until the marinade starts to brown. Set aside for 5 minutes before serving.

3 Mix the lemon juice, coriander and mint, then season. Toss with the salad leaves, mango and cucumber, then arrange on plates. Slice the lamb and serve over the salad.

NUTRITION PER SERVE Protein 30 g; **Fat 6.5 g**; Carbohydrate 8 g; Dietary Fibre 2 g; Cholesterol 90 mg; 965 kJ (230 cal)

Thai Beef Salad with Mint and Coriander

2 tablespoons dried shrimp
125 g (4 oz) English spinach
1 tablespoon sesame oil
500 g (1 lb) rump steak
1 cup (90 g/3 oz) bean sprouts
1 small red onion, thinly sliced
1 small red capsicum, cut into thin strips
1 small Lebanese cucumber, cut into thin strips
200 g (6$\frac{1}{2}$ oz) daikon radish, peeled and cut
into thin strips
1 small tomato, halved, seeded and thinly sliced
$\frac{1}{4}$ cup (5 g/$\frac{1}{4}$ oz) mint leaves
$\frac{1}{2}$ cup (15 g/$\frac{1}{2}$ oz) coriander leaves

2 cloves garlic, finely chopped
1–2 small red chillies, chopped
2 small green chillies, chopped

Dressing
$\frac{1}{4}$ cup (60 ml/2 fl oz) lime juice
$\frac{1}{4}$ cup (60 ml/2 fl oz) fish sauce
1 tablespoon finely chopped lemon grass
1 teaspoon sugar

PREPARATION TIME 40 minutes
TOTAL COOKING TIME 4 minutes
SERVES 6

1 Soak the dried shrimp in hot water for 15 minutes; drain well and chop finely. Wash the English spinach and drain well. Trim the thick stalks and coarsely shred the leaves.

2 Heat the oil in a frying pan, add the steak and cook over high heat for 1$\frac{1}{2}$–2 minutes on each side until medium-rare. Allow to cool slightly and then slice the steak thinly.

3 To make the dressing, combine the lime juice, fish sauce, lemon grass and sugar in a small jug. Whisk until the ingredients are well combined.

4 To assemble the salad, combine the shrimp, sliced beef, bean sprouts, onion, capsicum, cucumber, radish, tomato, mint, coriander, garlic and chillies in a large bowl. Place the spinach on a serving plate, top with the combined beef and vegetables, and drizzle with the dressing.

NUTRITION PER SERVE Protein 25 g; **Fat 6 g**; Carbohydrate 6 g; Dietary Fibre 4 g; Cholesterol 65 mg; 730 kJ (175 cal)

Won Ton Noodle Soup

70 g (2¼ oz) raw prawns
70 g (2¼ oz) veal mince
3 tablespoons soy sauce
1 tablespoon finely chopped spring onion
1 tablespoon finely chopped water chestnuts
1 teaspoon finely chopped ginger
2 cloves garlic, finely chopped
24 gow gee wrappers

1.25 litres (44 fl oz) chicken stock
2 tablespoons mirin
500 g (1 lb) baby bok choy, finely shredded
8 spring onions, sliced

PREPARATION TIME 25 minutes
TOTAL COOKING TIME 25 minutes
SERVES 4

1 Peel, devein and finely chop the prawns. Mix with the veal mince, 2 teaspoons soy sauce, spring onion, water chestnuts, ginger and garlic. Lay the round wrappers out on a work surface and place a teaspoon of mixture in the middle of each.

2 Moisten the edges of the wrappers and bring up the sides to form a pouch. Pinch together to seal. Cook in batches in a large pan of rapidly boiling water for 4–5 minutes. Drain and divide among soup bowls.

3 Bring the stock, remaining soy sauce and mirin to the boil in a pan. Add the bok choy, cover and simmer for 2 minutes, or until the bok choy has just wilted. Add the sliced spring onion and season. Ladle the stock, bok choy and spring onion over the won tons.

NUTRITION PER SERVE Protein 10 g; **Fat 5 g**; Carbohydrate 30 g; Dietary Fibre 5 g; Cholesterol 25 mg; 760 kJ (180 cal)

Mediterranean Fish Soup

1/2 teaspoon saffron threads
3 teaspoons oil
2 large onions, thinly sliced
1 leek, white part only, chopped
4 cloves garlic, finely chopped
1 bay leaf, torn
1/2 teaspoon dried marjoram
1 teaspoon grated orange rind
2 tablespoons dry white wine
1 red capsicum, cut into chunks
500 g (1 lb) tomatoes, chopped

1/2 cup (125 ml/4 fl oz) tomato purée
2 cups (500 ml/16 fl oz) fish stock
2 tablespoons tomato paste
2 teaspoons soft brown sugar
500 g (1 lb) firm white fish, cut into bite-sized pieces
3 tablespoons chopped fresh parsley

PREPARATION TIME 30 minutes
TOTAL COOKING TIME 45 minutes
SERVES 4

1 Soak the saffron in 2 tablespoons boiling water; set aside. Heat the oil in a large heavy-based pan, over low heat. Add the onion, leek, garlic, bay leaf and marjoram. Cover and cook for 10 minutes, shaking the pan occasionally, until the onion is soft. Add the rind, wine, capsicum and tomato, cover and cook for 10 minutes.

2 Stir in the purée, stock, tomato paste, sugar and saffron (with liquid). Bring to the boil, reduce the heat and simmer, uncovered, for 15 minutes.

3 Add the fish to the soup, cover and cook for 8 minutes, or until tender. Add salt and pepper and half the parsley. Garnish with parsley.

NUTRITION PER SERVE Protein 30 g; **Fat 7.5 g**; Carbohydrate 15 g; Dietary Fibre 5 g; Cholesterol 90 mg; 1020 kJ (245 cal)

Chicken and Couscous Soup

1 tablespoon olive oil
1 onion, sliced
½ teaspoon ground cumin
½ teaspoon paprika
1 teaspoon grated fresh ginger
1 clove garlic, crushed
2 celery sticks, sliced
2 small carrots, sliced
2 zucchini, sliced

1.25 (39 fl oz) litres chicken stock
2 chicken breast fillets, sliced
pinch saffron threads, optional
½ cup (95 g/3 oz) instant couscous
2 tablespoons chopped fresh parsley

PREPARATION TIME 25 minutes
TOTAL COOKING TIME 30 minutes
SERVES 6

1   Heat the oil in a large heavy-based pan. Add the onion and cook over medium heat for 10 minutes, or until very soft, stirring occasionally. Add the cumin, paprika, ginger and garlic and cook, stirring, for 1 minute further.

2   Add the celery, carrot and zucchini and stir to coat with the spices. Stir in the stock. Bring to the boil, then reduce the heat and simmer, partially covered, for about 15 minutes, or until the vegetables are tender.

3   Add the chicken and saffron to the pan and cook for about 5 minutes, or until the chicken is just tender; do not overcook. Stir in the couscous and chopped parsley and serve.

Hint

Add the couscous to the soup just before serving because it absorbs liquid quickly and becomes very thick.

NUTRITION PER SERVE Protein 19 g; **Fat 5.5 g**; Carbohydrate 12 g; Dietary Fibre 2 g; Cholesterol 37 mg; 712 kJ (170 cal)

Moroccan Lamb, Chickpea and Coriander Soup

165 g (³/₄ cup) dried chickpeas
1 tablespoon olive oil
850 g (1 lb 14 oz) boned lamb leg,
cut into 1 cm (¹/₂ inch) cubes
1 onion, chopped
2 garlic cloves, crushed
¹/₂ teaspoon ground cinnamon
¹/₂ teaspoon ground turmeric
¹/₂ teaspoon ground ginger
4 tablespoons chopped coriander (cilantro)

2 x 400 g (14 oz) cans chopped tomatoes
1 litre (4 cups) chicken stock
160 g (²/₃ cup) dried red lentils, rinsed
coriander (cilantro) leaves, to garnish

PREPARATION TIME 15 minutes + overnight
soaking
TOTAL COOKING TIME 2 hours 15 minutes
SERVES 4–6

1 Soak the chickpeas in cold water overnight. Drain, and rinse well.

2 Heat the oil in a large saucepan over high heat and brown the lamb in batches for 2–3 minutes. Reduce the heat to medium, return the lamb to the pan with the onion and garlic and cook for 5 minutes. Add the spices, season and cook for 2 minutes. Add the coriander, tomato, stock and 500 ml (2 cups) water and bring to the boil over high heat.

3 Add the lentils and chickpeas and simmer, covered, over low heat for 1 hour 30 minutes. Uncover and cook for 30 minutes, or until the lamb is tender and the soup is thick. Season. Garnish with coriander.

NUTRITION PER SERVE Protein 29 g; **Fat 9.5 g**; Carbohydrate 22 g; Dietary Fibre 7.5 g; Cholesterol 51 mg; 1200 kJ (285 Cal)

Hot and Sour Lime Soup with Beef

1 litre (4 cups) beef stock
2 stems lemon grass, white part only, halved
3 garlic cloves, halved
2.5 x 2.5 cm (1 inch x 1 inch) piece fresh
ginger, sliced
100 g (3½ oz) coriander (cilantro), leaves
and stalks separated
4 spring onions (scallions), thinly sliced on
the diagonal
2 strips lime zest
2 star anise

3 small red chillies, seeded and finely chopped
500 g (1 lb 2 oz) fillet steak, trimmed
2 tablespoons fish sauce
1 tablespoon grated palm sugar or
soft brown sugar
2 tablespoons lime juice
coriander (cilantro) leaves, extra, to garnish

PREPARATION TIME 20 minutes
TOTAL COOKING TIME 30 minutes
SERVES 4

1 Put the beef stock, lemon grass, garlic, ginger, coriander stalks, 2 spring onions, lime zest, star anise, 1 teaspoon chopped chilli and 1 litre (4 cups) water in a saucepan. Bring to a boil and simmer, covered, for 25 minutes. Strain and return the liquid to the pan.

2 Heat a ridged chargrill pan (griddle) until very hot. Brush lightly with olive oil and sear the steak on both sides until browned on the outside, but very rare in the centre.

3 Reheat the soup, adding the fish sauce and palm sugar. Season with salt and black pepper. Add the lime juice to taste (you may want more than 2 tablespoons)—you should achieve a hot and sour flavour.

4 Add the remaining spring onion and the chopped coriander leaves to the soup. Slice the beef across the grain into thin strips. Curl the strips into a decorative pattern, then place in the centre of four deep wide serving bowls. Pour the soup over the beef and garnish with the remaining chilli and a few extra coriander leaves.

NUTRITION PER SERVE Protein 31 g; **Fat 7 g**; Carbohydrate 7 g; Dietary Fibre 0.5 g; Cholesterol 84 mg; 900 kJ (215 Cal)

Mushroom, Ricotta and Olive Pizza

4 Roma tomatoes, quartered
¾ teaspoon caster sugar
7 g (¼ oz) dry yeast or
15 g (½ oz) fresh yeast
½ cup (125 ml/4 fl oz) skim milk
1¾ cups (220 g/7 oz) plain flour
2 teaspoons olive oil
2 cloves garlic, crushed
1 onion, thinly sliced

750 g (1½ lb) mushrooms, sliced
1 cup (250 g/8 oz) low-fat ricotta
2 tablespoons sliced black olives
small fresh basil leaves

PREPARATION TIME 30 minutes + proving
TOTAL COOKING TIME 1 hour
SERVES 6

1 Preheat the oven to hot 210°C (415°F/Gas 6–7). Put the tomato on a baking tray covered with baking paper, sprinkle with salt, cracked black pepper and ½ teaspoon sugar and bake for 20 minutes, or until the edges are starting to darken.

2 Stir the yeast and remaining sugar with 3 table-spoons warm water until the yeast dissolves. Cover and leave in a warm place until foamy. Warm the milk. Sift the flour into a large bowl and stir in the yeast and milk. Mix to a soft dough, then turn onto a lightly floured surface and knead for 5 minutes. Leave, covered, in a lightly oiled bowl in a warm place for 40 minutes, or until doubled in size.

3 Heat the oil in a pan and fry the garlic and onion until soft. Add the mushrooms and stir until they are soft and the liquid has evaporated. Leave to cool.

4 Turn the dough out onto a lightly floured surface and knead lightly. Roll out to a 36 cm (15 inch) circle and transfer to a lightly greased oven or pizza tray. Spread with the ricotta, leaving a border to turn over the filling. Top with the mushrooms, leaving a circle in the centre, and arrange the tomato and olives in the circle. Fold the dough edge over onto the mushroom and dust the edge with flour. Bake for 25 minutes, or until the crust is golden. Garnish with basil.

NUTRITION PER SERVE Protein 15 g; **Fat 7.5 g**; Carbohydrate 30g; Dietary Fibre 6 g; Cholesterol 20 mg; 1100 kJ (265 cal)

Polenta Pie

2 eggplants, thickly sliced
1⅓ cups (350 ml/11 fl oz) vegetable stock
1 cup (150 g/5 oz) fine polenta
½ cup (60 g/2 oz) finely grated Parmesan
1 tablespoon olive oil
1 large onion, chopped
2 cloves garlic, crushed
1 large red capsicum, diced
2 zucchini, thickly sliced

150 g (5 oz) button mushrooms, cut into quarters
400 g (13 oz) can chopped tomatoes
3 teaspoons balsamic vinegar
olive oil, for brushing

PREPARATION TIME 20 minutes + 15 minutes standing + refrigeration
TOTAL COOKING TIME 50 minutes
SERVES 6

1 Spread the eggplant in a single layer on a board and sprinkle with salt. Leave for 15 minutes, then rinse, pat dry and cut into cubes.

2 Line a 22 cm (9 inch) round cake tin with foil. Pour the stock and 1⅓ cups (350 ml/11 fl oz) water into a saucepan and bring to the boil. Add the polenta in a thin stream and stir over low heat for 5 minutes, or until the liquid is absorbed and the mixture comes away from the side of the pan.

3 Remove from the heat and stir in the cheese until it melts through the polenta. Spread into the prepared tin, smoothing the surface as much as possible. Refrigerate until set.

4 Preheat the oven to moderately hot 200°C (400°F/Gas 6). Heat the oil in a large saucepan with a lid and add the onion. Cook over medium heat, stirring occasionally, for 3 minutes, or until soft. Add the garlic and cook for a further 1 minute.

Add the eggplant, capsicum, zucchini, mushrooms and tomato. Bring to the boil, then reduce the heat and simmer, covered, for 20 minutes, or until the vegetables are tender. Stir occasionally to prevent catching on the bottom of the pan. Stir in the vinegar and season.

5 Transfer the vegetable mixture to a 22 cm (9 inch) ovenproof pie dish, piling it up slightly in the centre.

6 Turn out the polenta, peel off the foil and cut into 12 wedges. Arrange smooth-side-down in a single layer, over the vegetables—don't worry about any gaps. Brush lightly with a little olive oil and bake for 20 minutes, or until lightly brown and crisp.

NUTRITION PER SERVE Protein 8 g; **Fat 8.5 g**; Carbohydrate 23 g; Dietary Fibre 4.5 g; Cholesterol 8 mg; 855 kJ (205 cal)

Pasta with Grilled Capsicum

400 g (14 oz) pasta gnocchi
6 large red capsicums (peppers), halved
2 tablespoons olive oil
1 onion, thinly sliced
3 garlic cloves, finely chopped
2 tablespoons shredded basil

whole basil leaves, to garnish
shaved Parmesan cheese, to serve (optional)

PREPARATION TIME 15 minutes
TOTAL COOKING TIME 15 minutes
SERVES 4–6

1 Cook the pasta in a large pan of rapidly boiling salted water until al dente.

2 Cut the capsicums into large flattish pieces. Cook, skin-side-up, under a hot grill until the skin blackens and blisters. Put in a plastic bag and cool, then peel.

3 Heat the oil in a large frying pan, add the onion and garlic and cook over medium heat for 5 minutes, or until soft. Cut one capsicum into thin strips and add it to the onion mixture.

4 Chop the remaining capsicum, then purée in the food processor until smooth. Add to the onion mixture and cook over low heat for 5 minutes, or until warmed through.

5 Toss the sauce through the pasta. Season, then stir in the shredded basil. Garnish with basil leaves and serve with Parmesan if desired.

NUTRITION PER SERVE Protein 11 g; **Fat 7 g**; Carbohydrate 62 g; Dietary Fibre 4 g; Cholesterol 0 mg; 1515 kJ (360 Cal)

Scallops with Bok Choy

24 large scallops with corals
2 tablespoons light soy sauce
1 tablespoon fish sauce
1 tablespoon honey
1 tablespoon kecap manis
grated rind and juice of 1 lime
2 teaspoons grated fresh ginger
1 lime, cut into wedges, to garnish

Sesame bok choy
1 tablespoon sesame oil
1 tablespoon sesame seeds
1 clove garlic, crushed
8 baby bok choy, halved lengthways

PREPARATION TIME 10 minutes + marinating
TOTAL COOKING TIME 8 minutes
SERVES 4

1 Rinse the scallops, remove the dark vein and dry with paper towels. Combine the soy and fish sauce, honey, kecap manis, lime rind and juice and ginger. Pour over the scallops, cover and refrigerate for about 15 minutes. Drain and reserve the marinade.

2 To make the sesame bok choy, pour the oil onto a preheated chargrill pan or barbecue flatplate and add the sesame seeds and garlic. Cook, stirring, for 1 minute, or until the seeds are golden. Arrange the bok choy in a single layer on the hot plate and pour on the reserved marinade. Cook for 3–4 minutes, turning once, until tender. Remove and keep warm.

3 Wipe clean the hot plate, brush with some oil and reheat. Add the scallops and cook, turning, for about 2 minutes, or until they become opaque. Place the scallops on top of the sesame bok choy and serve with the lime wedges.

NUTRITION PER SERVE Protein 15 g; **Fat 5 g**; Carbohydrate 10 g; Dietary Fibre 1 g; Cholesterol 25 mg; 670 kJ (160 cal)

Mussels with Lemon Grass, Basil and Wine

1 kg (2 lb) black mussels
1 tablespoon oil
1 onion, chopped
4 cloves garlic, chopped
2 stems lemon grass, white part only, chopped
1–2 teaspoons chopped small red chillies
1 cup (250 ml/8 fl oz) white wine

1 tablespoon fish sauce
1 cup (30 g/1 oz) Thai basil leaves, roughly chopped

PREPARATION TIME 30 minutes
TOTAL COOKING TIME 15 minutes
SERVES 4–6

1 Scrub the mussels and debeard. Soak them in a bowl of cold water for 10 minutes; drain and discard any that are open and don't close when tapped on the work surface.

2 Heat the oil in a wok and stir-fry the onion, garlic, lemon grass and chilli over low heat for 4 minutes. Add the wine and fish sauce and cook for 3 minutes.

3 Add the mussels to the wok and toss well. Cover the wok; increase the heat and cook for 3–4 minutes or until the mussels open. Discard any that don't open. Add the chopped basil and toss well before serving.

Hint

Do not overcook the mussels or they will become tough. Use small fresh black mussels and buy a few extra, in case any are cracked, damaged or already open.

NUTRITION PER SERVE Protein 13 g; **Fat 5 g**; Carbohydrate 1.5 g; Dietary Fibre 0 g; Cholesterol 30 mg; 1271 kJ (302 cal)

Seafood and Herb Risotto

150 g (5 oz) white boneless fish fillet such
as sea perch
8 black mussels (200 g/6½ oz)
8 raw prawns (250 g/8 oz)
1.75 litres (61 fl oz) chicken stock
cooking oil spray
2 onions, finely chopped
2 cloves garlic, finely chopped
1 celery stick, finely chopped

2 cups (440 g/14 oz) arborio rice
2 tablespoons chopped fresh parsley
1 tablespoon chopped fresh oregano
1 tablespoon chopped fresh thyme leaves
2 tablespoons freshly grated Parmesan

PREPARATION TIME 40 minutes
TOTAL COOKING TIME 45–50 minutes
SERVES 4

1 Cut the fish fillet into small cubes. Scrub the mussels well and remove the beards. Discard any mussels that are not tightly closed. Peel and devein the prawns, leaving the tails intact. Put the seafood in a bowl and refrigerate until required.

2 Put the stock in a saucepan and bring to the boil, then reduce the heat until just gently simmering.

3 Lightly spray a large saucepan with cooking oil and heat over medium heat. Add the onion, garlic and celery and cook for 2–3 minutes. Add 2 tablespoons water, cover and cook for 5 minutes, or until the vegetables have begun to soften. Add the arborio rice as well as 2 tablespoons water, cover and continue to cook over medium heat for 3–4 minutes, or until the rice grains are well coated.

4 Gradually add ½ cup (125 ml/4 fl oz) of the hot stock to the rice mixture, stirring constantly over low heat with a wooden spoon, until all the stock has been absorbed. Repeat the process, adding ½ cup of liquid each time until all but a small amount of stock is left and the rice is just tender.

5 Meanwhile, bring a small amount of water to the boil in a saucepan. Add the mussels, cover and cook for about 3 minutes, shaking the pan occasionally, until the mussels have opened. Drain the mussels and discard any that have not opened. Set aside.

6 Add the fish and prawns and the remaining hot stock to the rice. Stir well and continue to cook for about 5–10 minutes, or until the seafood is just cooked and the rice is tender and creamy. Remove from the heat, add the cooked mussels, cover and set aside for 5 minutes. Stir the herbs and Parmesan through the risotto, then season well with freshly cracked pepper and salt. Serve immediately in individual bowls.

NUTRITION PER SERVE Protein 40 g; **Fat 5 g**; Carbohydrate 90 g; Dietary Fibre 4 g; Cholesterol 175 mg; 2395 kJ (570 cal)

Fish with Ginger

1 tablespoon peanut oil
1 small onion, finely sliced
3 teaspoons ground coriander
600 g (1 ¼ lb) boneless white fish fillets, such
as perch, sliced
1 tablespoon julienned fresh ginger
1 teaspoon finely chopped and seeded
green chilli

2 tablespoons lime juice
2 tablespoons coriander leaves

PREPARATION TIME 20 minutes
TOTAL COOKING TIME 15 minutes
SERVES 4

1 Heat a wok until very hot, add the oil and swirl to coat. Add the onion and stir-fry for 4 minutes, or until soft and golden. Add the ground coriander and cook for 1–2 minutes, or until the mixture is fragrant.

2 Add the fish, ginger and chilli, and stir-fry for 5–7 minutes, or until the fish is cooked through. Stir in the lime juice and season. Garnish with the coriander leaves and serve.

NUTRITION PER SERVE Protein 30 g; **Fat 9 g**; Carbohydrate 1 g; Dietary Fibre 0.4 g; Cholesterol 105 mg; 895 kJ (214 cal)

Tuna with Potato Ratatouille

3 tablespoons olive oil
1 teaspoon grated lemon zest
4 garlic cloves, crushed
4 x 175 g (6 oz) pieces of tuna
1 red onion, thinly sliced
350 g (¾ lb) fennel, thinly sliced
125 ml (½ cup) dry white wine
830 g (1 lb 13 oz) canned chopped tomatoes
600 g (1 lb 5 oz) new potatoes, quartered

350 g (¾ lb) zucchini (courgettes), cut into 1.5 cm (⅝ inch) rounds
2 tablespoons lemon juice
2 tablespoons chopped parsley
sprigs of fennel, to garnish

PREPARATION TIME 15 minutes
TOTAL COOKING TIME 1 hour
SERVES 4

1 Combine 1 tablespoon of the oil with the lemon zest and half the garlic. Place the tuna in a flat dish and cover with the marinade. Refrigerate.

2 Heat 1 tablespoon oil in a saucepan, add the onion and cook for 5 minutes, or until soft. Add the fennel and remaining garlic and cook, stirring, over low heat for 15–20 minutes, or until softened. Increase the heat to medium, stir in the white wine and cook for 2 minutes.

3 Add the tomato and potato, bring to a boil, then reduce the heat and simmer for 20 minutes, or until the potato is tender. Add the zucchini and cook for 5 minutes, or until tender. Season and stir in the parsley. Remove from the heat and keep warm.

4 Heat the remaining oil in a large non-stick frying pan. Cook the tuna for 1–2 minutes each side. Add the lemon juice and cook for 20–30 seconds. Remove from the pan, cool slightly and cut into 2 cm (¾ inch) slices. Serve the ratatouille with the tuna slices over the top. Garnish with the fennel sprigs.

NUTRITION PER SERVE Protein 38 g; **Fat 5 g**; Carbohydrate 33 g; Dietary Fibre 10 g; Cholesterol 50 mg; 1400 kJ (333 Cal)

Crumbed Fish with Wasabi Cream

¾ cup (60 g/2 oz) fresh breadcrumbs
¾ cup (25 g/¾ oz) cornflakes
1 sheet nori, torn roughly
¼ teaspoon paprika
4 x 150 g (5 oz) pieces firm white fish fillets
plain flour, for dusting
1 egg white
1 tablespoon skim milk
1 spring onion, thinly sliced

Wasabi cream
½ cup (125 ml/4 oz) low-fat natural yoghurt
1 teaspoon wasabi (see NOTE)
1 tablespoon light mayonnaise
1 teaspoon lime juice

PREPARATION TIME 25 minutes + 15 minutes refrigeration
TOTAL COOKING TIME 20 minutes
SERVES 4

1 Preheat the oven to moderate 180°C (350°F/Gas 4). Combine the crumbs, cornflakes, nori and paprika in a food processor and process until the nori is finely chopped.

2 Dust the fish lightly with plain flour, dip into the combined egg white and milk, then into the breadcrumb mixture. Press the crumb mixture on firmly, then refrigerate for 15 minutes.

3 Line a baking tray with non-stick baking paper and put the fish on the paper. Bake for 15–20 minutes, or until the fish flakes easily when tested with a fork.

4 To make the wasabi cream, mix the ingredients thoroughly in a bowl. Serve a spoonful on top of the fish and sprinkle with spring onion.

Note
Wasabi paste (a pungent paste, also known as Japanese horseradish) and nori (sheets of paper-thin dried seaweed) are both available from Japanese food stores.

NUTRITION PER SERVE Protein 35 g; **Fat 6 g**; Carbohydrate 25 g; Dietary Fibre 1 g; Cholesterol 105 mg; 1270 kJ (305 cal)

Chilli Chicken Stir-fry

375 g (12 oz) Hokkien noodles
4 chicken thigh fillets, cut into small pieces (see NOTE)
1–2 tablespoons sweet chilli sauce
2 teaspoons fish sauce
1 tablespoon oil
100 g (3½ oz) baby sweet corn, halved lengthways

150 g (5 oz) sugar snap peas, topped and tailed
1 tablespoon lime juice

PREPARATION TIME 10 minutes
TOTAL COOKING TIME 10 minutes
SERVES 6

1 Place the noodles in a large bowl, cover with boiling water and gently break apart with a fork. Leave for 5 minutes, then drain.

2 Combine the chicken, sweet chilli sauce and fish sauce in a bowl.

3 Heat a wok or frying pan over high heat, add the oil and swirl to coat. Add the chicken pieces and stir-fry for 3–5 minutes, or until cooked through. Then add the corn and sugar snap peas and stir-fry for 2 minutes. Add the noodles and lime juice and serve.

Note
If thigh fillets are unavailable, use 3 breast fillets.

NUTRITION PER SERVE Protein 30 g; **Fat 6.5 g**; Carbohydrate 50 g; Dietary Fibre 4 g; Cholesterol 53 mg; 1593 kJ (380 cal)

Ginger Chicken with Black Fungus

3 tablespoons black fungus (see NOTE)
1 tablespoon oil
3 cloves garlic, chopped
5 cm (2 inches) ginger, shredded
500 g (1 lb) chicken breast fillets, sliced
4 spring onions, chopped
1 tablespoon Golden Mountain sauce
1 tablespoon fish sauce

2 teaspoons brown sugar
½ red capsicum, finely sliced
½ cup (15 g/½ oz) coriander leaves
½ cup (30 g/1 oz) shredded Thai basil leaves

PREPARATION TIME 25 minutes
TOTAL COOKING TIME 15 minutes
SERVES 4

1 Place the fungus in a bowl of hot water for 15 minutes until it is soft and swollen; drain and chop roughly.

2 Heat the oil in a large wok and stir-fry the garlic and ginger for 1 minute. Add the chicken in batches, stir-frying over high heat until it is cooked. Return all the chicken to the wok. Add the onions and Golden Mountain sauce and cook for 1 minute.

3 Add the fish sauce, brown sugar and fungus to the wok. Toss well, cover and steam for 2 minutes. Serve immediately, scattered with red capsicum, coriander and basil.

Note
Black fungus is a dried mushroom that swells to many times its size when soaked in hot water. It is available from Asian food speciality stores and is also known as 'wood ear' or 'cloud ear' mushroom.

NUTRITION PER SERVE Protein 6 g; **Fat 5 g**; Carbohydrate 4.5 Dietary Fibre 1 g; Cholesterol 8.5 mg; 359 kJ (86 cal)

Soy Chicken and Crispy Noodles

750 g (1 ½ lb) chicken thigh fillets
3 teaspoons cornflour
⅓ cup (80 ml/2¾ fl oz) soy sauce oil, for
deep-frying
100 g (3½ oz) dried rice vermicelli
1 clove garlic, crushed
2 teaspoons grated fresh ginger
1 carrot, sliced
2 celery sticks, sliced

1 red capsicum, sliced
1 green capsicum, sliced
100 g (3½ oz) snow peas, trimmed
6 spring onions, sliced
¼ cup (60 ml/2 fl oz) chicken stock

PREPARATION TIME 30 minutes
TOTAL COOKING TIME 30 minutes
SERVES 4–6

1 Cut the chicken into 2 cm (¾ inch) cubes. Mix the cornflour into half the soy sauce; add the chicken, then cover and refrigerate until ready to use.

2 Heat the oil in a large pan. Break the vermicelli into small pieces. Drop a noodle into the oil: if it fizzes and puffs, the oil is hot enough. Add the noodles in small amounts and cook until puffed and white. Drain on paper towels and set aside.

3 Heat 1 tablespoon of oil in a wok, add the chicken and stir-fry in batches over high heat for about 4 minutes, or until cooked. Remove the chicken from the wok and set aside.

4 Heat 1 tablespoon of oil in the wok and cook the garlic and ginger for 30 seconds. Add the vegetables and cook, tossing well, for 2–3 minutes.

5 Add the chicken, stock and remaining soy sauce, and stir until boiled and thickened. Transfer to the centre of serving plates and arrange the noodles around the edge.

NUTRITION PER SERVE Protein 30 g; **Fat 9 g**; Carbohydrate 20 g; Dietary Fibre 2 g; Cholesterol 85 mg; 1150 kJ (275 cal)

Pasta with Artichokes and Chargrilled Chicken

1 tablespoon olive oil
3 chicken breast fillets
500 g (1 lb) pasta
8 slices prosciutto
280 g (9 oz) jar artichokes in oil, drained and
quartered, oil reserved
150 g (5 oz) semi-dried tomatoes, thinly sliced

90 g (3 oz) baby rocket leaves
2–3 tablespoons balsamic vinegar

PREPARATION TIME 10 minutes
TOTAL COOKING TIME 30 minutes
SERVES 6

1 Lightly brush a chargrill or frying pan with the oil and heat over high heat. Cook the chicken for 6–8 minutes each side, or until cooked through. Thinly slice and set aside.

2 Cook the pasta in a large pan of rapidly boiling salted water until al dente. Drain and return to the pan to keep warm. Meanwhile, place the prosciutto on a grill tray and cook under a hot grill for 2 minutes each side, or until crisp. Cool slightly and break into pieces. Combine the pasta with the chicken, prosciutto, artichokes, tomato and rocket in a bowl and toss. Whisk together ¼ cup (60 ml/2 fl oz) of the reserved artichoke oil and the balsamic vinegar and toss through the pasta mixture. Season and serve.

NUTRITION PER SERVE Protein 30 g; **Fat 9 g**; Carbohydrate 51 g; Dietary Fibre 4 g; Cholesterol 103 mg; 1705 kJ (410 cal)

Steamed Lemon Grass and Ginger Chicken with Asian greens

200 g (6½ oz) fresh egg noodles
4 chicken breast fillets
2 stems lemon grass
5 cm (2 inch) piece fresh ginger, cut into
julienne strips
1 lime, thinly sliced
2 cups (500 ml/16 fl oz) chicken stock
1 bunch (350 g/12 oz) choy sum, cut into
10 cm (4 inch) lengths
800 g (1 lb 10 oz) Chinese broccoli, cut into
10 cm (4 inch) lengths

3 tablespoons kecap manis
3 tablespoons soy sauce
1 teaspoon sesame oil
toasted sesame seeds, to garnish

PREPARATION TIME 25 minutes
TOTAL COOKING TIME 40 minutes
SERVES 4

1 Cook the egg noodles in a saucepan of boiling water for 5 minutes, then drain and keep warm.

2 Cut each chicken breast fillet horizontally through the middle so that you are left with eight thin flat chicken fillets.

3 Cut the lemon grass into lengths that are about 5 cm (2 inches) longer than the chicken fillets, then cut in half lengthways. Place one piece of lemon grass onto one half of each chicken breast fillet, top with some ginger and lime slices, then top with the other half of the fillet.

4 Pour the stock into a wok and bring to a simmer. Place two of the chicken fillets in a paper-lined bamboo steamer. Place the steamer over the wok and steam over the simmering stock for 12–15 minutes, or until the chicken is tender. Remove the chicken from the steamer, cover and keep warm. Repeat with the other fillets.

5 Steam the greens in the same way for 3 minutes, or until tender. Bring the stock in the wok to the boil.

6 Place the kecap manis, soy sauce and sesame oil in a bowl and whisk together well.

7 Divide the noodles among four serving plates and ladle the boiling stock over them. Top with a pile of Asian greens, then add the chicken and generously drizzle each serve with the sauce. Sprinkle with toasted sesame seeds and serve.

NUTRITION PER SERVE Protein 65 g; **Fat 7.5 g**; Carbohydrate 37 g; Dietary Fibre 9 g; Cholesterol 119 mg; 2045 kJ (488 cal)

Orange and Rosemary Glazed Chicken

2 seedless oranges
1/2 cup (185 g/6 oz) honey
2 tablespoons Dijon mustard
1 1/2 tablespoons chopped fresh rosemary
4 cloves garlic, crushed
1.5 kg (3 lb) chicken pieces

PREPARATION TIME 10 minutes + 4 hours marinating
TOTAL COOKING TIME 50 minutes
SERVES 6

1 Squeeze the juice from one orange into a bowl, add the honey, Dijon mustard, rosemary and garlic and mix together well. Cut the other orange in half and then cut it into slices.

2 Add the chicken and orange slices to the orange juice mixture. Season and mix well and leave to marinate for at least 4 hours. Preheat the oven to moderately hot 200°C (400°F/Gas 6). Line a large baking tray with foil. Arrange the chicken and the marinade in the baking tray.

3 Bake for 40–50 minutes, or until the chicken is golden, turning once and basting with the marinade.

NUTRITION PER SERVE Protein 40 g; **Fat 8.5 g**; Carbohydrate 27 g; Dietary Fibre 1 g; Cholesterol 138 mg; 1470 kJ (350 cal)

Barbecued Garlic Chicken

6 cloves garlic, crushed
1 1/2 tablespoons cracked black peppercorns
1/2 cup (25 g/3/4 oz) chopped fresh coriander
leaves and stems
4 coriander roots, chopped
1/3 cup (80 ml/2 3/4 fl oz) lime juice
1 teaspoon soft brown sugar
1 teaspoon ground turmeric
2 teaspoons light soy sauce
4 chicken breast fillets

Salad
1 small green cucumber, unpeeled
1 large Roma tomato
1/4 small red onion, thinly sliced
1 small red chilli, finely chopped
2 tablespoons fresh coriander leaves
2 tablespoons lime juice
1 teaspoon soft brown sugar
1 tablespoon fish sauce

PREPARATION TIME 20 minutes + marinating
TOTAL COOKING TIME 10 minutes
SERVES 4

1 Blend the garlic, peppercorns, coriander, lime juice, sugar, turmeric and soy sauce in a food processor until smooth. Transfer to a bowl.

2 Remove the tenderloins from the chicken fillets. Score the top of each fillet three times. Add the fillets and tenderloins to the marinade, cover and refrigerate for 2 hours or overnight, turning the chicken occasionally.

3 To make the salad, halve the cucumber and scoop out the seeds with a teaspoon. Cut into slices. Halve the tomato lengthways and slice. Combine the cucumber, tomato, onion, chilli and coriander in a small bowl. Drizzle with the combined lime juice, sugar and fish sauce.

4 Cook the chicken on a lightly greased barbecue hotplate for 3 minutes on each side, or until tender. Serve the chicken immediately with the salad.

NUTRITION PER SERVE Protein 52 g; **Fat 5.5 g**; Carbohydrate 6 g; Dietary Fibre 2 g; Cholesterol 110 mg; 1195 kJ (285 cal)

Ham and Herb Mushrooms

8 large flat field mushrooms
3 spring onions, finely chopped
150 g (5 oz) smoked ham, finely chopped
$3/4$ cup (60 g/2 oz) fresh breadcrumbs
2 tablespoons finely grated Parmesan
1 tablespoon chopped fresh parsley

2 teaspoons chopped fresh oregano
2 tablespoons olive oil

PREPARATION TIME 15 minutes
TOTAL COOKING TIME 5 minutes
SERVES 4

1 Remove the stalks from the mushrooms and finely chop them. In a bowl, combine the mushroom stalks with the spring onion, ham, breadcrumbs, Parmesan, parsley and oregano. Season with salt and freshly ground black pepper and add a little water to bring the mixture together.

2 Divide the mixture among the mushroom caps and brush lightly with the olive oil.

3 Brush a preheated chargrill pan or barbecue flatplate with a little olive oil and cook the mushrooms, filling-side-up, for about 3 minutes. Cover loosely with foil and allow to steam for another 2 minutes.

NUTRITION PER SERVE Protein 7 g; **Fat 5 g**; Carbohydrate 6 g; Dietary Fibre 1 g; Cholesterol 10 mg; 415 kJ (98 cal)

Linguine with Bacon, Mushrooms and Peas

3 bacon rashers
2 teaspoons olive oil
2–3 cloves garlic, crushed
1 red onion, chopped
185 g (6 oz) field mushrooms, sliced
1/3 cup (20 g/3/4 oz) chopped fresh parsley
1 cup (150 g/5 oz) peas
1 1/2 cups (375 ml/12 fl oz) low-fat light
evaporated milk

2 teaspoons cornflour
325 g (11 oz) linguine
25 g (3/4 oz) Parmesan shavings

PREPARATION TIME 20 minutes
TOTAL COOKING TIME 25 minutes
SERVES 4

1 Remove the fat and rind from the bacon and chop roughly. Heat the oil in a medium pan, add the garlic, onion and bacon and cook over low heat for 5 minutes, stirring frequently, until the onion and bacon are soft. Add the sliced mushrooms and cook, stirring, for another 5 minutes, or until soft.

2 Add the parsley, peas and milk to the pan. Mix the cornflour with 1 tablespoon of water until smooth, add to the mixture and stir over medium heat until slightly thickened.

3 Cook the pasta in a large pan of rapidly boiling salted water until al dente. Drain well and serve with the hot sauce and Parmesan shavings.

Note
Parmesan adds a nice flavour to this dish, but leave it out if you are wanting a meal with a very low fat content.

NUTRITION PER SERVE Protein 30 g; **Fat 7 g**; Carbohydrate 80 g; Dietary Fibre 9 g; Cholesterol 25 mg; 2085 kJ (500 cal)

Pork Stew with Asian Flavours

2 teaspoons olive oil
2 cloves garlic, crushed
1 tablespoon julienned fresh ginger
1 teaspoon Sichuan pepper, crushed
1 star anise
800 g (1 lb 10 oz) pork fillet, cut into
3 cm (1 1/4 inch) cubes
1 cup (250 ml/8 fl oz) chicken stock
1 tablespoon light soy sauce

1 tablespoon cornflour
2 teaspoons chilli bean paste
250 g (8 oz) Chinese broccoli, cut into
4 cm (1 1/2 inch) lengths

PREPARATION TIME 20 minutes
TOTAL COOKING TIME 50 minutes
SERVES 4

1   Heat the olive oil in a heavy-based saucepan over high heat. Add the garlic, ginger, Sichuan pepper and star anise and cook for 30 seconds, or until fragrant. Stir in the pork to coat.

2   Add the stock, soy sauce and 1 cup (250 ml/ 8 fl oz) water to the pan and bring to the boil. Reduce the heat and simmer for 40 minutes, or until the pork is tender. Combine the cornflour with 2 tablespoons of the cooking liquid, stirring until smooth. Add to the pan and stir over medium heat for 3–4 minutes, or until the mixture thickens slightly.

3   Stir in the bean paste and Chinese broccoli and cook for a further 2 minutes, or until the broccoli is just tender. Serve with steamed rice.

NUTRITION PER SERVE Protein 47 g; **Fat 7 g**; Carbohydrate 4 g; Dietary Fibre 3 g; Cholesterol 190 mg; 1135 kJ (270 Cal)

Pork and Eggplant Pot

olive oil spray, for cooking
375 g (12 oz) slender eggplant, cut into 3 cm (1 1/4 inch) slices
8 bulb spring onions
400 g (14 oz) can chopped tomatoes
2 cloves garlic, crushed
2 teaspoons ground cumin
500 g (1 lb) pork fillet, sliced 3 cm (1 1/4 inch) thick

plain flour, seasoned with salt and freshly ground pepper
2/3 cup (170 ml/5 1/2 fl oz) cider
1 sprig of rosemary
2 tablespoons finely chopped toasted almonds

PREPARATION TIME 20 minutes
TOTAL COOKING TIME 1 hour 20 minutes
SERVES 4

1 Spray some olive oil into a large saucepan. Brown the eggplant in batches over high heat, adding oil as needed. Remove. Quarter the spring onions. Add some oil to the pan and fry over medium heat for 5 minutes. Add the tomatoes, garlic and cumin and cook for 2 minutes. Remove.

2 Coat the pork in the flour, shaking off any excess. Brown in batches over medium-high heat until golden, adding oil as needed. Remove.

3 Add the cider to the pan and stir-well, scraping down the side and base. Allow to boil for 1–2 minutes, then add 1/2 cup (125 ml) water. Reduce the heat and stir in the spring onions and tomato. Add the pork, season and stir the rosemary sprig into the stew. Partially cover and simmer gently for 20 minutes. Layer the eggplant on top, partially cover and cook for 25 minutes, or until the pork is tender. Just before serving, gently toss in the almonds.

NUTRITION PER SERVE Protein 30 g; **Fat 7 g**; Carbohydrate 10 g; Dietary Fibre 5 g; Cholesterol 60 mg; 980 kj (235 cal)

Lamb Chops with Citrus Pockets

4 lamb chump chops, about 250 g
(8 oz) each
2 tablespoons lemon juice

Citrus filling
3 spring onions, finely chopped
1 celery stick, finely chopped
2 teaspoons grated fresh ginger

¾ cup (60 g/2 oz) fresh breadcrumbs
2 tablespoons orange juice
2 teaspoons finely grated orange rind
1 teaspoon chopped fresh rosemary

PREPARATION TIME 25 minutes
TOTAL COOKING TIME 15 minutes
SERVES 4

1 Cut a deep, long pocket in the side of each lamb chop.

2 Mix together all the filling ingredients and spoon into the pockets in the lamb.

3 Cook on a hot, lightly oiled barbecue flatplate or grill, turning once, for 15 minutes, or until the lamb is cooked through but still pink in the centre. Drizzle with the lemon juice.

NUTRITION PER SERVE Protein 35 g; **Fat 5 g**; Carbohydrate 15 g; Dietary Fibre 1 g; Cholesterol 105 mg; 1080 kJ (335 cal)

Lamb with Borlotti Beans

1 cup (200 g/6½ oz) dried borlotti beans
1 tablespoon olive oil
12 lamb loin chops
1 onion, finely chopped
1 celery stick, chopped
1 carrot, chopped
3 cloves garlic, finely chopped
½ teaspoon dried chilli flakes
1 teaspoon cumin seeds

2 cups (500 ml/16 fl oz) lamb or chicken stock
2 bay leaves
3 tablespoons lemon juice
⅓ cup (20 g/¾ oz) chopped fresh parsley
1 tablespoon shredded fresh mint

PREPARATION TIME 20 minutes + overnight soaking
TOTAL COOKING TIME 2 hours
SERVES 6

1 Soak the beans overnight in cold water. Drain, rinse well and set aside.

2 Preheat the oven to moderate 180°C (350°F/Gas 4). Heat the oil in a large heavy-based pan. Brown the lamb over high heat in batches and transfer to a casserole dish.

3 Add the onion, celery and carrot to the pan and cook over low heat for about 10 minutes, or until soft and golden. Add the garlic, chilli and cumin seeds and cook for 1 minute, then transfer to the casserole dish.

4 Add the stock, beans and bay leaves. Cover tightly; bake for 1½– 1¾ hours, or until the lamb is very tender and the beans are cooked. Season well and stir in the lemon juice, parsley and mint just before serving.

NUTRITION PER SERVE Protein 30 g; **Fat 8 g**; Carbohydrate 20 g; Dietary Fibre 5 g; Cholesterol 65 mg; 1185 kJ (280 cal)

Veal Cutlets in Chilli Tomato Sauce

5 slices wholemeal bread
3 tablespoons fresh parsley
3 cloves garlic
4 thick veal cutlets, trimmed
3 tablespoons skim milk
2 teaspoons olive oil
1 onion, finely chopped
1 tablespoon capers, drained
1 teaspoon canned green peppercorns, chopped

1 teaspoon chopped red chilli
2 tablespoons balsamic vinegar
1 teaspoon soft brown sugar
2 tablespoons tomato paste
440 g (14 oz) can chopped tomatoes

PREPARATION TIME 35 minutes
TOTAL COOKING TIME 35 minutes
SERVES 4

1 Preheat the oven to moderate 180°C (350°F/Gas 4). Place a rack in a small baking dish. Chop the bread, parsley and garlic in a food processor to make fine breadcrumbs.

2 Season the cutlets on both sides with salt and black pepper. Pour the milk into a bowl and put the breadcrumbs on a plate. Dip the veal in the milk, then coat in the crumbs, pressing the crumbs on. Transfer to the rack and bake for 20 minutes.

3 Meanwhile, heat the oil in a small pan over medium heat. Add the onion, capers, peppercorns and chilli, cover and cook for 8 minutes. Stir in the vinegar, sugar and tomato paste and stir until boiling. Stir in the tomato, reduce the heat and simmer for 15 minutes. Season, to taste.

4 Remove the cutlets from the rack and wipe the dish. Place about three-quarters of the tomato sauce in the base and put the cutlets on top. Spoon the remaining sauce over the cutlets and return to the oven. Reduce the oven to slow 150°C (300°F/Gas 2), then bake for another 10 minutes, or until heated through. Sprinkle with extra chopped parsley to garnish.

NUTRITION PER SERVE Protein 15 g; **Fat 6 g**; Carbohydrate 20 g; Dietary Fibre 5 g; Cholesterol 25 mg; 845 kJ (200 cal)

Penne with Veal Ragout

2 onions, sliced
2 bay leaves, crushed
1.5 kg (3 lb) veal shin, cut into osso buco pieces
(see NOTE)
1 cup (250 ml/8 fl oz) red wine
2 x 400 g (13 oz) cans crushed tomatoes
1 1/2 cups (375 ml/12 fl oz) beef stock

2 teaspoons chopped fresh rosemary
400 g (13 oz) penne
1 cup (150 g/5 oz) frozen peas

PREPARATION TIME 15 minutes
TOTAL COOKING TIME 2 hours 40 minutes
SERVES 4

1 Preheat the oven to hot 220°C (425°F/Gas 7). Scatter the onion over the bottom of a large roasting tin, lightly spray with oil and place the bay leaves and veal pieces on top. Season with salt and pepper. Roast for 10–15 minutes, or until the veal is browned. Take care that the onion doesn't burn.

2 Pour the wine over the veal and return to the oven for a further 5 minutes. Reduce the heat to moderate 180°C (350°F/Gas 4), remove the tin from the oven and pour on the tomato, stock and 1 teaspoon of the rosemary. Cover with foil and return to the oven. Cook for 2 hours, or until the veal is starting to fall from the bone. Remove the foil and cook for a further 15 minutes, or until the meat loosens away from the bone and the liquid has evaporated slightly.

3 Cook the pasta in a large pan of rapidly boiling salted water until al dente. Drain and return to the pan to keep warm. Meanwhile, remove the veal from the oven and cool slightly. Add the peas and remaining rosemary and place over a hotplate. Cook over medium heat for 5 minutes, or until the peas are cooked. Serve the pasta topped with the ragout.

Note

Most butchers sell veal shin cut into osso buco pieces. If sold in a whole piece, ask the butcher to cut it for you (the pieces are about 3–4 cm (1 1/4-1 1/2 inch) thick). It is also available at some supermarkets. You can either remove the meat from the bone before serving, or leave it on.

NUTRITION PER SERVE Protein 52 g; **Fat 5 g**; Carbohydrate 81 g; Dietary Fibre 10 g; Cholesterol 125 mg; 2605 kJ (620 cal)

Steak in Red Wine

750 g (1½ lb) rump steak
1 cup (250 ml/8 fl oz) good red wine
2 teaspoons garlic salt
1 tablespoon dried oregano leaves
cracked black pepper

PREPARATION TIME 10 minutes + 3 hours marinating
TOTAL COOKING TIME 10 minutes
SERVES 4

1 Trim the steak of any fat. Mix together the wine, salt, oregano and pepper. Put the steak in a shallow, non-metallic dish and add the marinade. Toss well, cover and refrigerate for at least 3 hours.

2 Cook the steak on a hot, lightly oiled barbecue flatplate or grill for 3–4 minutes on each side, brushing frequently with the marinade.

Hint
Choose a basting brush with pure bristles. Nylon bristles can melt in the heat of the barbecue.

NUTRITION PER SERVE Protein 44 g; **Fat 5 g**; Carbohydrate 0 g; Dietary Fibre 0 g; Cholesterol 126 mg; 1100 kJ (264 cal)

Beef Bourguignon

1 kg (2 lb) topside or round steak
plain flour, seasoned with salt and pepper
3 rashers bacon, rind removed
1 tablespoon oil
12 pickling onions
1 cup (250 ml/8 fl oz) red wine
2 cups (500 ml/16 fl oz) beef stock

1 teaspoon dried thyme
200 g (6½ oz) button mushrooms
2 bay leaves

PREPARATION TIME 10 minutes
TOTAL COOKING TIME 2 hours
SERVES 6

1 Trim the steak of fat and sinew and cut into 2 cm (¾ inch) cubes. Lightly toss in the seasoned flour to coat, shaking off the excess.

2 Cut the bacon into 2 cm (¾ inch) squares. Heat the oil in a large pan and quickly cook the bacon over medium heat. Remove the bacon from the pan, then add the meat and brown well in batches. Remove and set aside. Add the onions to the pan and cook until golden.

3 Return the bacon and meat to the pan with the remaining ingredients. Bring to the boil, reduce the heat and simmer, covered, for 1½ hours, or until the meat is very tender, stirring now and then. Remove the bay leaves to serve.

Storage
Refrigerate in an airtight container for up to 3 days.

NUTRITION PER SERVE Protein 40 g; **Fat 7 g**; Carbohydrate 5 g; Dietary Fibre 1 g; Cholesterol 90 mg; 1150 kJ (275 cal)

Passionfruit Tart

³⁄₄ cup (90 g/3 oz) plain flour
2 tablespoons icing sugar
2 tablespoons custard powder
30 g (1 oz) butter
3 tablespoons light evaporated milk

Filling
¹⁄₂ cup (125 g/4 oz) ricotta
1 teaspoon vanilla essence
¹⁄₄ cup (30 g/1 oz) icing sugar

2 eggs, lightly beaten
4 tablespoons passionfruit pulp
(about 8 passionfruit)
³⁄₄ cup (185 ml/6 fl oz) light evaporated milk

PREPARATION TIME 25 minutes + 30 minutes refrigeration
TOTAL COOKING TIME 1 hour
SERVES 8

1 Preheat the oven to 200°C (400°F/ Gas 6). Lightly spray a 22 cm (9 inch) loose-based flan tin with oil. Sift the flour, icing sugar and custard powder into a bowl and rub in the butter until crumbs form. Add enough evaporated milk to form a soft dough. Bring together on a floured surface until just smooth. Gather into a ball, wrap in plastic and chill for 15 minutes.

2 Roll the pastry out on a floured surface to fit the tin, then refrigerate for 15 minutes. Cover with baking paper and fill with rice or dried beans. Bake for 10 minutes, remove the rice or beans and paper and bake for another 5–8 minutes, or until golden. Allow to cool. Reduce the oven to warm 160°C (315°F/Gas 2–3).

3 Beat the ricotta with the vanilla essence and icing sugar until smooth. Add the eggs, passionfruit pulp and milk, then beat well. Put the tin with the pastry case on a baking tray and pour in the filling. Bake for 40 minutes, or until set. Cool in the tin. Dust with icing sugar to serve.

NUTRITION PER SERVE Protein 8 g; **Fat 6.5 g**; Carbohydrate 25 g; Dietary Fibre 3 g; Cholesterol 65 mg; 750 kJ (180 cal)

Mocha Cheesecake

50 g (1 ½ oz) plain sweet biscuits
¼ cup (30 g/1 oz) walnuts
30 g (1 oz) butter, melted
1 tablespoon instant coffee
2 teaspoons cocoa powder
1 tablespoon gelatine powder
250 g (8 oz) low-fat ricotta
½ cup (125 g/4 oz) caster sugar

1 cup (250 ml/ 8 fl oz) reduced-fat evaporated milk, well chilled
cocoa powder, extra, for dusting

PREPARATION TIME 30 minutes +
4 hours 30 minutes refrigeration
TOTAL COOKING TIME Nil
SERVES 8

1 Line the base of a 22 cm (9 inch) springform tin with baking paper. Place the biscuits and walnuts in a food processor, and process until finely crushed. Add the melted butter and pulse until well combined. Press the biscuit and nut mixture into the base of the prepared tin and chill for 30 minutes.

2 Mix the coffee, cocoa, gelatine and ½ cup (125 ml) boiling water in a heatproof bowl. Place the bowl in a saucepan of very hot water, and stir until the gelatine has dissolved and the mixture is smooth. Cool slightly.

3 Beat the ricotta and sugar together with electric beaters for 2 minutes, or until the sugar dissolves. Gradually beat in the coffee mixture.

4 Place the evaporated milk in a separate bowl and beat with electric beaters on high speed for 1 minute, or until the mixture is very frothy and holds its shape. Beat in the mocha ricotta mixture until well combined.

5 Pour over the biscuit base. Cover with plastic wrap and refrigerate for 3–4 hours, or until set. To serve, wrap a wrung-out hot tea towel around the tin for 1 minute, then run a flat-bladed knife around the inside of the tin and remove the collar. Dust with cocoa and serve with raspberries, if desired.

Note
Make sure all the ingredients are at a similar temperature before combining.

NUTRITION PER SERVE Protein 9 g; **Fat 9.5 g**; Carbohydrate 20 g; Dietary Fibre 0.5 g; Cholesterol 26.5 mg; 825 kJ (195 Cal)

Tiramisu

3 tablespoons custard powder
1 cup (250 ml/8 fl oz) skim milk
2 tablespoons caster sugar
2 teaspoons vanilla essence
2 x 130 g (4½ oz) tubs low-fat fromage frais
or light vanilla Fruche
2 egg whites
1⅔ cups (410 ml/13 fl oz) prepared strong
coffee, cooled

2 tablespoons amaretto
250 g (8 oz) Savoyardi (sponge finger) biscuits
2 tablespoons unsweetened dark cocoa powder

PREPARATION TIME 15 minutes + overnight
refrigeration
TOTAL COOKING TIME 5 minutes
SERVES 6

1 Stir the custard powder in a small pan with 2 tablespoons of the milk until dissolved. Add the remaining milk, sugar and vanilla and stir over medium heat until the mixture boils and thickens. Remove from the heat. This custard will be thicker than the usual custard. Transfer to a bowl, cover the surface with plastic wrap and cool at room temperature.

2 Using electric beaters, mix the custard and the fromage frais in a bowl. Beat for 2 minutes. In a small bowl, whip the egg whites until soft peaks form, then fold into the custard mixture.

3 Pour the coffee into a dish and add the amaretto. Quickly dip the biscuits, one at a time, in the coffee mixture, just enough to cover (dip quickly, or they'll be soggy) and arrange in a single layer over the base of a 2.75 litre (96 fl oz) dish.

4 Using half the cream mixture, smooth it evenly over the biscuits. Dust half the dark cocoa over the cream and then repeat the layers with the remaining biscuits and cream. Cover with plastic wrap. Refrigerate overnight, or for at least 6 hours. Dust with dark cocoa powder to serve.

NUTRITION PER SERVE Protein 5 g; **Fat 5.5 g**; Carbohydrate 26 g; Dietary Fibre 1 g; Cholesterol 7.5 mg; 754 kJ (180 cal)

Lemon Meringue Pie

Lemon filling
$1/3$ cup (40 g/$1 1/4$ oz) cornflour
2 tablespoons plain flour
$1 1/2$ cups (375 g/12 oz) caster sugar
1 tablespoon golden syrup
3 teaspoons grated lemon rind
$1/2$ cup (125 ml/4 fl oz) lemon juice
6 egg yolks

Crust
canola oil spray
3 tablespoons reduced-fat dairy spread

1 tablespoon honey
200 g ($6 1/2$ oz) flaked corn cereal, finely crushed

Meringue
6 egg whites
$1 1/2$ cups (375 g/12 oz) caster sugar
$1/2$ teaspoon cornflour

PREPARATION TIME 25 minutes + cooling
TOTAL COOKING TIME 30 minutes
SERVES 8

1 To make the filling, place the cornflour, flour and sugar in a heavy-based saucepan. Gradually stir in $1 1/2$ cups (375 ml) hot water, and stir over low heat until combined and the sugars have dissolved. Add the golden syrup, then stir in the lemon rind and lemon juice. Increase the heat to medium–high and cook, stirring, for 5–6 minutes, or until the mixture boils and thickens, then cook for 1 minute more. Reduce the heat and, using a whisk, incorporate the egg yolks one at a time, whisking until smooth. Remove from the heat, cover the surface with plastic wrap and cool completely.

2 Preheat the oven to moderately hot 190°C (375°F/Gas 5). Lightly spray a 22 cm (9 inch) pie tin with canola spray. To make the crust, melt the dairy spread and honey in a small saucepan. Place the crushed cereal in a bowl, pour in the melted dairy spread mixture and mix together well. Press into the base and side of the prepared tin and neaten the upper edges. Bake for 8–9 minutes, or until the edges just start to brown. Remove from the oven and cool. Reduce the oven temperature to moderate 180°C (350°F/Gas 4).

3 To make the meringue, whisk the egg whites in a clean, dry bowl until soft peaks form. Gradually add the sugar and whisk until stiff peaks form, then whisk in the cornflour. To assemble, spread the filling evenly over the pie shell. Spoon the meringue over the top, covering the filling completely. Form peaks in the meringue with the back of the spoon. Bake for 7–8 minutes, or until the meringue is set and golden brown. Serve hot or cold with whipped light cream or low-fat ice cream.

NUTRITION PER SERVE Protein 7 g; **Fat 7.5 g**; Carbohydrate 100 g; Dietary Fibre 1 g; Cholesterol 141.5 mg; 2015 kJ (480 cal)

Rhubarb and Pear Crumble

600 g (1 1/4 lb) rhubarb
2 strips lemon rind
1 tablespoon honey, or to taste
2 firm, ripe pears
1/2 cup (50 g/1 3/4 oz) rolled oats
1/4 cup (35 g/1 1/4 oz) wholemeal plain flour

1/3 cup (60 g/2 oz) soft brown sugar
50 g (1 3/4 oz) butter

PREPARATION TIME 20 minutes
TOTAL COOKING TIME 35 minutes
SERVES 6

1 Trim the rhubarb, wash and cut into 3 cm (1 1/4 inch) pieces. Place in a medium pan with the lemon rind and 1 tablespoon water. Cook, covered, over low heat for 10 minutes, or until tender. Cool a little. Stir in the honey and remove the lemon rind.

2 Preheat the oven to moderate 180°C (350°F/Gas 4). Peel, core and cut the pears into 2 cm (3/4 inch) cubes and combine with the rhubarb. Pour into a 1.25 litre (44 fl oz) dish and smooth the surface.

3 To make the topping, combine the oats, flour and brown sugar in a bowl. Rub in the butter with your fingertips until the mixture is crumbly. Spread over the fruit. Bake for 15 minutes, or until cooked and golden.

NUTRITION PER SERVE Protein 3.5 g; **Fat 8 g**; Carbohydrate 30 g; Dietary Fibre 6 g; Cholesterol 0 mg; 885 kJ (210 cal)

10-15 g

Tangy Prawn and Noodle Salad

Dressing
2 cloves garlic, crushed
1 small fresh red chilli, chopped
1 tablespoon oil
2 tablespoons fish sauce
3 tablespoons lime juice
1 teaspoon shrimp paste
20 g ($\frac{1}{2}$ oz) grated palm sugar or soft brown sugar
100 g ($3\frac{1}{2}$ oz) cellophane noodles

4 spring onions, sliced
375 g (12 oz) cooked prawns, peeled and deveined
$\frac{1}{3}$ cup (10 g/$\frac{1}{3}$ oz) chopped fresh coriander leaves
2 tablespoons salted beer nuts, chopped

PREPARATION TIME 20 minutes
TOTAL COOKING TIME 10 minutes
SERVES 4

1 Combine all the dressing ingredients, stirring well to dissolve the sugar. Set aside.

2 Cook the noodles in plenty of boiling water for 10 minutes, or until tender. Rinse, drain, and cut into shorter lengths.

3 Add the dressing to the noodles and mix well. Toss in the spring onions, prawns and coriander, transfer to serving bowls and sprinkle with nuts. Serve at room temperature.

NUTRITION PER SERVE Protein 30 g; **Fat 10 g**; Carbohydrate 10 g; Dietary Fibre 4 g; Cholesterol 180 mg; 1080 kJ (255 cal)

Warm Chicken Salad

500 g (1 lb) chicken thigh fillets, fat removed
2 teaspoons Thai red curry paste
1 teaspoon chopped red chilli
1 clove garlic, crushed
1 stem fresh lemon grass (white part only),
finely chopped
cooking oil spray
1 red onion, thinly sliced
2 tomatoes, cut in wedges
1/2 cup (25 g/3/4 oz) chopped fresh mint
1/4 cup (15 g/1/2 oz) chopped fresh coriander
400 g (13 oz) mixed salad leaves
2 tablespoons roasted peanuts

Dressing
1 1/2 tablespoons soft brown sugar
2 tablespoons fish sauce
2 tablespoons lime juice
2 kaffir lime leaves, shredded
2 teaspoons oil

PREPARATION TIME 30 minutes + overnight
marinating
TOTAL COOKING TIME 20 minutes
SERVES 4

1   Cut the chicken into thin strips and mix with the curry paste, chilli, garlic and lemon grass. Cover and refrigerate for several hours or overnight.

2   Lightly spray a non-stick frying pan with oil and cook the chicken in batches until tender and lightly browned; set aside. Add the onion to the pan and cook for 1 minute, or until just soft. Return the chicken and any juices to the pan and add the tomato, mint and coriander, stirring until heated. Set aside until just warm.

3   To make the dressing, thoroughly mix the ingredients in a jug. In a large bowl, toss the chicken mixture with the salad leaves and dressing and serve. Sprinkle with the peanuts.

NUTRITION PER SERVE Protein 25 g; **Fat 10 g**; Carbohydrate 15 g; Dietary Fibre 2.5 g; Cholesterol 50 mg; 1050 kJ (250 cal)

Thai Pork Tenderloin and Green Mango Salad

2 stems lemon grass (white part only), thinly sliced
1 garlic clove
2 red Asian shallots
1 tablespoon coarsely chopped fresh ginger
1 red bird's-eye chilli, seeded
1 tablespoon fish sauce
15 g (½ cup) coriander (cilantro) leaves
1 teaspoon grated lime zest
1 tablespoon lime juice
2 tablespoons oil
2 pork tenderloins, trimmed

Dressing
1 large red chilli, seeded and finely chopped
2 garlic cloves, finely chopped
3 coriander (cilantro) roots, finely chopped
1 tablespoon grated palm sugar or soft brown sugar

2 tablespoons fish sauce
3 tablespoons lime juice

Salad
2 green mangoes or 1 small green papaya, peeled and cut into julienne strips
1 carrot, grated
45 g (½ cup) bean sprouts
½ red onion, thinly sliced
3 tablespoons chopped mint
3 tablespoons chopped coriander (cilantro)
3 tablespoons chopped Vietnamese mint

PREPARATION TIME 45 minutes + 2 hours refrigeration
TOTAL COOKING TIME 10 minutes
SERVES 6

1 Place the lemon grass, garlic, shallots, ginger, chilli, fish sauce, coriander, lime zest, lime juice and oil in a blender or food processor and process until a coarse paste forms. Transfer to a non-metallic dish. Coat the pork in the marinade, cover and refrigerate for at least 2 hours, but no longer than 4 hours.

2 To make the salad dressing, mix all the ingredients together in a bowl.

3 To make the salad, combine all the salad ingredients in a large bowl.

4 Preheat a grill or chargrill pan (griddle) and cook the pork over medium heat for 4–5 minutes each side, or until cooked through. Remove from the heat and rest for 5 minutes before slicing.

5 Toss the dressing and salad together. Season to taste with salt and cracked black pepper. Arrange the sliced pork in a circle in the centre of each plate and top with salad. To make this a main course, serve with steamed jasmine rice, if desired.

NUTRITION PER SERVE Protein 60 g; **Fat 14 g**; Carbohydrate 20 g; ; Dietary Fibre 3 g; Cholesterol 122 mg; 1860 kJ (444 Cal)

Pesto Beef Salad

100 g (3½ oz) button mushrooms
1 large yellow capsicum
1 large red capsicum
cooking oil spray
100 g (3½ oz) lean fillet steak
1½ cups (135 g/4½ oz) penne

Pesto
1 cup (50 g/1¾ oz) fresh basil leaves, tightly packed
2 cloves garlic, chopped
2 tablespoons pepitas (pumpkin seeds)
1 tablespoon olive oil
2 tablespoons orange juice
1 tablespoon lemon juice

PREPARATION TIME 30 minutes
TOTAL COOKING TIME 25 minutes
SERVES 4

1 Cut the mushrooms into quarters. Cut the capsicums into quarters, discarding the seeds and membrane. Grill the capsicum, skin-side-up, until the skins blacken and blister. Cool under a damp tea towel, then peel and dice the flesh.

2 Spray a non-stick frying pan with oil and cook the steak over high heat for 3–4 minutes each side. Remove and leave for 5 minutes before cutting into thin slices. Season with a little salt.

3 To make the pesto, finely chop the basil leaves, garlic and pepitas in a food processor. With the motor running, add the oil, lemon and orange juice. Season with salt and pepper.

4 Meanwhile, cook the penne in a large pan of rapidly boiling salted water until al dente. Drain, then toss with the pesto in a large bowl.

5 Add the capsicum pieces, steak slices and mushroom quarters to the penne and toss to distribute evenly. Serve immediately.

NUTRITION PER SERVE Protein 15 g; **Fat 10 g**; Carbohydrate 30 g; Dietary Fibre 4 g; Cholesterol 15 mg; 1330 kJ (270 cal)

Tofu and Asian Mushroom Noodle Soup

2 dried Chinese mushrooms
10 g (¼ oz) dried black fungus
1 tablespoon vegetable oil
6 spring onions (scallions), thickly sliced
on the diagonal
1 red chilli, seeded and chopped
60 g (2¼ oz) oyster mushrooms, sliced
60 g (2¼ oz) Swiss brown mushrooms, sliced
1½ tablespoons dashi granules
3 tablespoons light soy sauce
1½ tablespoons mirin

125 g (4½ oz) dried wheat noodles
200 g (7 oz) water spinach or spinach, cut into
4 cm (1½ inch) slices
300 g (10½ oz) firm tofu, cut into
2 cm (¾ inch) cubes
10 g (⅓ cup) coriander (cilantro) leaves

PREPARATION TIME 20 minutes
COOKING TIME 15 minutes
SERVES 4

1 Soak the Chinese mushrooms in 250 ml (1 cup) hot water to soften. Squeeze dry and reserve the liquid. Discard the stalks and finely chop the caps. Cover the black fungus in hot water and soak until soft. Drain.

2 Heat the oil in a large saucepan or wok. Cook the Chinese mushrooms, black fungus, spring onion and chilli over high heat for 1 minute. Add the oyster and Swiss brown mushrooms and cook for 2 minutes.

3 Stir in the dashi granules, soy sauce, mirin, reserved mushroom liquid and 1.5 litres (6 cups) water. Bring to the boil, then stir in the noodles. Cook over medium heat for 5 minutes, or until soft.

4 Add the water spinach and cook for 2 minutes, then add the tofu and coriander. Serve at once.

Note

Dashi granules can be bought at Japanese shops and at some supermarkets. Water spinach can be bought at Asian grocery shops.

NUTRITION PER SERVE Protein 17 g; **Fat 10.5 g**; Carbohydrate 26 g; Dietary Fibre 5.5 g; Cholesterol 0 mg; 1105 kJ (265 cal)

Lentil and Silverbeet Soup

280 g (1 1/2 cups) brown lentils, washed
1 litre (4 cups) chicken stock
850 g (1 lb 14 oz) silverbeet
3 tablespoons olive oil
1 large onion, finely chopped
4 garlic cloves, crushed
25 g (1/2 cup) finely chopped coriander

4 tablespoons lemon juice
lemon wedges, to serve

PREPARATION TIME 15 minutes
TOTAL COOKING TIME 1 hour 10 minutes
SERVES 6

1 Put the lentils in a large saucepan with the stock and 1 litre (4 cups) water. Bring to the boil, then reduce the heat and simmer, covered, for 1 hour.

2 Remove the stems from the silverbeet and shred the leaves. Heat the oil in a saucepan over medium heat and cook the onion for 2–3 minutes, or until transparent. Add the garlic and cook for 1 minute. Add the silverbeet and toss for 2–3 minutes, or until wilted. Stir the mixture into the lentils.

3 Add the chopped coriander and the lemon juice, then season and cover. Simmer for 15–20 minutes. Serve with the lemon wedges.

NUTRITION PER SERVE Protein 38 g; **Fat 15 g**; Carbohydrate 20 g; Dietary Fibre 11 g; Cholesterol 83 mg; 1782 kJ (425 Cal)

Chicken and Vegetable Soup

1.5 kg (3 lb) chicken
2 carrots, roughly chopped
2 celery sticks, roughly chopped
1 onion, quartered
4 fresh parsley sprigs
2 bay leaves
4 black peppercorns
50 g (1¾ oz) butter
2 tablespoons plain flour
2 potatoes, chopped
250 g (8 oz) butternut pumpkin, cut into bite-sized pieces
2 carrots, extra, cut into matchsticks

1 leek, cut into matchsticks
3 celery sticks, extra, cut into matchsticks
100 g (3½ oz) green beans, cut into short lengths, or baby green beans, halved
200 g (6½ oz) broccoli, cut into small florets
100 g (3½ oz) sugar snap peas, trimmed
50 g (1¾ oz) English spinach leaves, shredded
½ cup (125 ml/4 fl oz) cream
¼ cup (15 g/½ oz) chopped fresh parsley

PREPARATION TIME 1 hour + refrigeration
TOTAL COOKING TIME 1 hour 25 minutes
SERVES 6–8

1 Place the chicken in a large pan with the carrot, celery, onion, parsley, bay leaves, 2 teaspoons of salt and the peppercorns. Add 3 litres of water. Bring to the boil, then reduce the heat and simmer for 1 hour, skimming the surface as required. Allow to cool for at least 30 minutes. Strain and reserve the liquid.

2 Remove the chicken and allow to cool until it is cool enough to handle. Discard the skin, then cut or pull the flesh from the bones and shred into small pieces. Set the chicken meat aside.

3 Heat the butter in a large pan over medium heat and, when foaming, add the flour. Cook, stirring, for 1 minute. Remove from the heat and gradually stir in the stock. Return to the heat and bring to the boil, stirring constantly. Add the potato, pumpkin and extra carrot and simmer for 7 minutes. Add the leek, extra celery and beans and simmer for a further 5 minutes. Finally, add the broccoli and sugar snap peas and cook for a further 3 minutes.

4 Just before serving, add the chicken, spinach, cream and chopped parsley. Reheat gently but do not allow the soup to boil. Keep stirring until the spinach has wilted. Season to taste with salt and freshly ground black pepper. Serve the soup immediately.

Hint
Do not overcook the vegetables. They should be tender yet crispy.

NUTRITION PER SERVE Protein 50 g; **Fat 15 g**; Carbohydrate 15 g; Dietary Fibre 6 g; Cholesterol 130 mg; 1700 kJ (400 Cal)

Chicken and Spinach Risoni Soup

1 tablespoon olive oil
1 leek, quartered lengthways and thinly sliced
2 garlic cloves, crushed
1 teaspoon ground cumin
1.5 litres (6 cups) chicken stock
2 chicken breast fillets (about 200 g/7 oz each)
200 g (1 cup) risoni (see NOTE)

150 g (5½ oz) baby English spinach leaves, roughly chopped
1 tablespoon chopped dill
2 teaspoons lemon juice

PREPARATION TIME 15 minutes
TOTAL COOKING TIME 35 minutes
SERVES 4

1 Heat the oil in a large saucepan over a low heat. Add the leek and cook for 8–10 minutes, or until soft. Add the garlic and cumin and cook for 1 minute. Pour the chicken stock into the pan, increase the heat to high and bring to the boil. Reduce the heat to low, add the chicken fillets and simmer, covered, for 8 minutes. Remove the chicken from the broth with a slotted spoon, allow it to cool slightly, then shred it into small pieces.

2 Stir the risoni into the broth and simmer for 12 minutes, or until al dente.

3 Return the chicken to the broth, and add the chopped spinach and dill. Simmer for 2 minutes, or until the spinach has wilted.

4 Just before serving, stir in the lemon juice and season to taste with salt and freshly ground black pepper.

Note
Risoni is a rice-shaped pasta that is usually used in soups.

NUTRITION PER SERVE Protein 38 g; **Fat 13.5 g**; Carbohydrate 39 g; Dietary Fibre 3.5 g; Cholesterol 82.5 mg; 1815 kJ (435 cal)

Spinach Pie

1.5 kg (3 lb) English spinach
2 teaspoons olive oil
1 onion, chopped
4 spring onions, chopped
750 g (1 1/2 lb) reduced-fat
cottage cheese
2 eggs, lightly beaten
2 cloves garlic, crushed
pinch of ground nutmeg

1/4 cup (15 g/1/2 oz) chopped fresh mint
8 sheets filo pastry
30 g (1 oz) butter, melted
1/2 cup (40 g/1 1/4 oz) fresh breadcrumbs

PREPARATION TIME 25 minutes
TOTAL COOKING TIME 45 minutes
SERVES 6

1 Preheat the oven to moderate 180°C (350°F/ Gas 4). Lightly spray a square 1.5 litre (52 fl oz) capacity ovenproof dish with oil. Trim and wash the spinach, then place in a large pan. Cover and cook for 2–3 minutes, until the spinach is just wilted. Drain, cool then squeeze dry and chop.

2 Heat the oil in a small pan. Add the onion and spring onion and cook for 2–3 minutes, until softened. Combine in a bowl with the chopped spinach. Stir in the cottage cheese, egg, garlic, nutmeg and mint. Season and mix together thoroughly.

3 Brush a sheet of filo pastry with a little butter. Fold in half widthways and line the base and sides of the dish. Repeat with 3 more sheets. Keep the unused sheets moist by covering with a damp tea towel.

4 Sprinkle the breadcrumbs over the pastry. Spread the filling into the dish. Fold over any overlapping pastry. Brush and fold another sheet and place on top. Repeat with 3 more sheets. Tuck the pastry in at the sides. Brush the top with any remaining butter. Score squares or diamonds on top using a sharp knife. Bake for 40 minutes, or until golden. Cut the pie into squares to serve.

NUTRITION PER SERVE Protein 35 g; **Fat 10 g**; Carbohydrate 30 g; Dietary Fibre 8 g; Cholesterol 75 mg; 1500 kJ (360 cal)

Stuffed Eggplants

$\frac{1}{3}$ cup (60 g/2 oz) brown lentils
2 large eggplants
cooking oil spray
1 red onion, chopped
2 cloves garlic, crushed
1 red capsicum, finely chopped
$\frac{1}{3}$ cup (40 g/1$\frac{1}{3}$ oz) pine nuts, toasted
$\frac{3}{4}$ cup (140 g/4$\frac{1}{2}$ oz) cooked
short-grain rice

440 g (14 oz) can chopped tomatoes
2 tablespoons chopped fresh coriander
1 tablespoon chopped fresh parsley
2 tablespoons grated Parmesan

PREPARATION TIME 20 minutes
TOTAL COOKING TIME 1 hour
SERVES 4

1 Simmer the brown lentils in a pan of water for 25 minutes, or until soft; drain. Slice the eggplants in half lengthways and scoop out the flesh, leaving a 1 cm ($\frac{1}{2}$ inch) shell. Chop the flesh finely.

2 Spray a deep, large non-stick frying pan with oil, add 1 tablespoon water to the pan, then add the onion and garlic and stir until softened. Add the cooked lentils to the pan with the capsicum, pine nuts, rice, tomato and eggplant flesh. Stir over medium heat for 10 minutes, or until the eggplant has softened. Add the fresh coriander and parsley. Season, then toss until well mixed.

3 Cook the eggplant shells in boiling water for 4–5 minutes, or until tender, or microwave on High (100%) for 8 minutes. Spoon the filling into the eggplant shells and sprinkle with the Parmesan. Grill for 5–10 minutes, or until golden. Serve immediately.

NUTRITION PER SERVE Protein 15 g; **Fat 10 g**; Carbohydrate 50 g; Dietary Fibre 8.5 g; Cholesterol 9.5 mg; 1490 kJ (355 cal)

Asian Mushroom Risotto

10 g (¼ oz) dried Chinese mushrooms
2 cups (500 ml/16 fl oz) vegetable stock
2 tablespoons soy sauce
⅓ cup (80 ml/2¾ fl oz) mirin
150 g (5 oz) Swiss brown mushrooms
150 g (5 oz) oyster mushrooms
100 g (3½ oz) fresh shiitake mushrooms
150 g (5 oz) shimeji mushrooms
1 tablespoon butter
1 tablespoon olive oil
1 onion, finely chopped

3 cloves garlic, crushed
1 tablespoon finely chopped fresh ginger
2 cups (440 g/14 oz) arborio rice
100 g (3½ oz) enoki mushrooms, trimmed
2 tablespoons snipped fresh chives
shaved Parmesan, to garnish

PREPARATION TIME 20 minutes + 20 minutes soaking
TOTAL COOKING TIME 45 minutes
SERVES 4

1 Put the Chinese mushrooms in a bowl, cover with 2½ cups (625 ml/20 fl oz) hot water and soak for 20 minutes, then drain, reserving the liquid. Remove the stems and thinly slice the caps.

2 Heat the vegetable stock, soy sauce, mirin, reserved mushroom liquid and 1 cup (250 ml/ 8 fl oz) water in a large saucepan. Bring to the boil, then keep at a low simmer, skimming off any scum that forms on the surface.

3 Trim and slice the Swiss brown, oyster and shiitake mushrooms, discarding any woody ends. Trim the shimeji and pull apart into small clumps. Melt the butter in a large saucepan over medium heat, add all the mushrooms except the Chinese and enoki and cook, stirring, for 3 minutes, or until wilted, then remove from the pan.

4 Add the oil to the pan, then add the chopped onion and cook, stirring, for 4–5 minutes, or until soft and just starting to brown. Add the garlic and ginger and stir well until fragrant. Add the rice and stir for 1 minute, or until it is well coated in the oil mixture.

5 Gradually add ½ cup (125 ml/4 fl oz) of the hot stock to the rice. Stir constantly over medium heat until nearly all the liquid has been absorbed. Continue adding more stock, a little at a time, stirring for 20–25 minutes, until all the stock has been absorbed and the rice is tender.

6 Add all the mushrooms and stir well. Season and garnish with the chives and shaved Parmesan.

NUTRITION PER SERVE Protein 17 g; **Fat 15 g**; Carbohydrate 92 g; Dietary Fibre 8 g; Cholesterol 28 mg; 2397 kJ (573 cal)

Deep-fried Tofu with Hokkien Noodles

100 g (3½ oz) deep-fried tofu puffs
(see HINT)
2 tablespoons oil
1 onion, sliced
1 red capsicum, cut into squares
3 cloves garlic, crushed
2 teaspoons grated fresh ginger
¾ cup (120 g/4 oz) small chunks
fresh pineapple

500 g (1 lb) thin Hokkien noodles, gently
pulled apart
¼ cup (60 ml/2 fl oz) pineapple juice
¼ cup (60 ml/2 fl oz) hoisin sauce
¼ cup (15 g/½ oz) roughly chopped fresh
coriander

PREPARATION TIME 10 minutes
TOTAL COOKING TIME 5 minutes
SERVES 4

1 Slice the tofu puffs into three, then cut each slice into two or three pieces.

2 Heat the wok until very hot, add the oil and stir-fry the onion and capsicum for 1–2 minutes, or until beginning to soften. Add the garlic and ginger, stir-fry for 1 minute, then add the tofu and stir-fry for 2 minutes.

3 Add the pineapple chunks and noodles and toss until the mixture is combined and heated through. Add the pineapple juice, hoisin sauce and chopped coriander and toss to combine. Serve immediately.

Hint
Deep-fried tofu puffs are available from the refrigerated section in Asian grocery stores and some supermarkets. They have a very different texture to ordinary tofu.

NUTRITION PER SERVE Protein 10 g; **Fat 15 g**; Carbohydrate 65 g; Dietary Fibre 3.5 g; Cholesterol 0 mg; 1830 kJ (435 cal)

Vegetable and Noodle Stir-fry

350 g (¾ lb) fresh Hokkien (egg) noodles
1 teaspoon sesame oil
2 tablespoons vegetable oil
1 red onion, halved and thinly sliced
3 garlic cloves, crushed
3 x 3 cm (1¼ x 1¼ inch) piece fresh ginger, julienned
5 spring onions (scallions), cut into 5 cm (2 inch) lengths
1 small red chilli, seeded and finely chopped
3 star anise
1 small red capsicum (pepper), thinly sliced
100 g (3½ oz) snow peas (mangetout), trimmed and halved diagonally

100 g (3½ oz) open cap mushrooms, quartered
500 g (1 lb 2 oz) baby bok choy (pak choi), trimmed, leaves separated, cut into 5 cm (2 inch) lengths
115 g (¼ lb) baby corn, halved diagonally
2 teaspoons cornflour (cornstarch)
100 ml (3½ fl oz) Chinese barbecue sauce (char sui)
2 tablespoons Chinese rice wine (see NOTE)
15 g (½ cup) coriander (cilantro) leaves

PREPARATION TIME 25 minutes
TOTAL COOKING TIME 10 minutes
SERVES 4

1 Put the noodles in a large heatproof bowl, cover with boiling water and soak for 5 minutes. Use a fork to gently separate the noodles, then drain well. Toss with the sesame oil.

2 Heat a wok over high heat. Add the vegetable oil and swirl to coat. Add the red onion, garlic, ginger, spring onion and chilli and stir-fry for 1 minute. Add the star anise, capsicum, snow peas, mushrooms, bok choy and baby corn and stir-fry for 2–3 minutes.

3 Mix the cornflour with 1 teaspoon cold water. Add to the wok with the barbecue sauce and Chinese rice wine. Bring to the boil and cook for 1 minute, or until the ingredients are coated and the sauce thickens slightly. Stir in the coriander leaves and serve immediately.

Note
Chinese rice wine can be bought from Asian food stores and some large supermarkets. Otherwise you can use dry sherry.

NUTRITION PER SERVE Protein 14 g; **Fat 12.5 g**; Carbohydrate 69 g; Dietary Fibre 7.5 g; Cholesterol 11.5 mg; 1880 kJ (450 cal)

Fettucine Boscaiola

500 g (1 lb) button mushrooms
1 large onion
1 tablespoon olive oil
2 cloves garlic, finely chopped
2 x 425 g (14 oz) cans tomatoes,
roughly chopped

500 g (1 lb) fettucine
2 tablespoons chopped fresh parsley

PREPARATION TIME 20 minutes
TOTAL COOKING TIME 25 minutes
SERVES 6

1 Wipe the mushrooms with a damp paper towel and then slice finely, including the stems.

2 Chop the onion roughly. Heat the oil in a heavy-based frying pan and cook the onion and garlic over medium heat, stirring occasionally, for about 6 minutes, or until the vegetables are light golden. Add the tomato including the juice, along with the mushrooms, to the pan and bring the mixture to the boil. Reduce the heat, cover the pan and simmer for 15 minutes.

3 While the sauce is cooking, cook the fettucine in a large pan of rapidly boiling salted water until al dente. Drain and return to the pan.

4 Stir the parsley into the sauce and season well with salt and pepper. Toss the sauce through the pasta.

NUTRITION PER SERVE Protein 15 g; **Fat 10 g**; Carbohydrate 65 g; Dietary Fibre 10 g; Cholesterol 0 mg; 1640 kJ (390 cal)

Tagliatelle with Sweet Tomato and Walnut Sauce

4 ripe Roma tomatoes
1 tablespoon oil
1 onion, finely chopped
1 celery stalk, finely chopped
1 carrot, grated
2 tablespoons chopped fresh parsley
1 teaspoon red wine vinegar
¼ cup (60 ml/2 fl oz) white wine

500 g (1 lb) tagliatelle or fettucine
1 tablespoon olive oil, extra
¾ cup (90 g/3 oz) walnuts, roughly chopped
grated Parmesan, for serving

PREPARATION TIME 20 minutes
TOTAL COOKING TIME 45 minutes
SERVES 4–6

1 Score a cross on the bottom of each tomato, place in boiling water for 1 minute, then plunge into cold water. Peel the skin away from the cross and roughly chop the tomatoes.

2 Heat oil in a large heavy-based pan and cook the onion and celery for 5 minutes over low heat, stirring regularly. Add the tomatoes, carrot, parsley and combined vinegar and wine. Reduce the heat and simmer for 25 minutes. Season to taste.

3 Meanwhile, cook the pasta in a large pan of rapidly boiling salted water until al dente. Drain and return to the pan to keep warm.

4 Heat the extra oil in a frying pan and stir the walnuts over low heat for 5 minutes. Toss the pasta and sauce together and serve topped with walnuts and Parmesan cheese.

NUTRITION PER SERVE Protein 13 g; **Fat 10 g**; Carbohydrate 61 g; Dietary Fibre 6 g; Cholesterol 7 mg; 1654 kJ (395 cal)

Garlic and Ginger Prawns

2 tablespoons oil
1 kg (2 lb) raw king prawns, peeled, deveined
and butterflied, tails left intact
3–4 cloves garlic, finely chopped
5 cm (2 inch) piece fresh ginger, cut
into matchsticks
2–3 small red chillies, seeded and
finely chopped
6 coriander roots, finely chopped, plus a few
leaves to garnish

8 spring onions, cut into short lengths
1/2 red capsicum, thinly sliced
2 tablespoons lemon juice
1/2 cup (125 ml/4 fl oz) white wine
2 teaspoons crushed palm sugar
2 teaspoons fish sauce

PREPARATION TIME 25 minutes
TOTAL COOKING TIME 10 minutes
SERVES 4

1 Heat the wok until very hot, add the oil and swirl to coat. Stir-fry the prawns, garlic, ginger, chilli and coriander root in two batches for 1–2 minutes over high heat, or until the prawns turn pink. Remove all the prawns from the wok and set aside.

2 Add the spring onion and capsicum to the wok. Cook over high heat for 2–3 minutes. Add the lemon juice, wine and palm sugar. Cook until the liquid has reduced by two thirds.

3 Add the prawns and sprinkle with fish sauce. Toss to heat through. Garnish with coriander to serve.

NUTRITION PER SERVE Protein 1 g; **Fat 10 g**; Carbohydrate 4.5 g; Dietary Fibre 1.5 g; Cholesterol 0 mg; 550 kJ (130 cal)

Garlic Calamari with Parmesan

350 g (11½ oz) fresh calamari tubes, cleaned
4 cloves garlic, chopped
2 tablespoons olive oil
2 tablespoons finely chopped fresh parsley
1 large tomato, peeled, seeded and
finely chopped
¼ cup (25 g/1 oz) freshly grated Parmesan

PREPARATION TIME 30 minutes + 10 minutes
marinating
TOTAL COOKING TIME 5 minutes
SERVES 2–4

1 Cut the calamari tubes in half lengthways, wash and pat dry. Lay them flat, with the soft, fleshy side facing upwards, and cut into rectangular pieces, about 6 x 2.5cm (2¼ x 1 inch). Finely honeycomb by scoring the fleshy side with diagonal strips, one way and then the other, to create a diamond pattern.

2 Mix the garlic, oil, half the parsley, salt and pepper in a bowl. Add the calamari and refrigerate for at least 10 minutes.

3 Heat a lightly oiled chargrill pan or barbecue flatplate until very hot. Cook the calamari in 2 batches, tossing regularly, until they turn white. Add the chopped tomato and toss through to just heat.

4 Arrange the calamari on a plate and scatter with the Parmesan and remaining parsley.

NUTRITION PER SERVE (4) Protein 20 g; **Fat 15 g**; Carbohydrate 2 g; Dietary Fibre 1 g; Cholesterol 180 mg; 800 kj (190 cal)

Paella

500 g (1 lb) raw prawns
300 g (10 oz) skinless firm white fish fillets
250 g (8 oz) black mussels
200 g (6½ oz) calamari rings
2 tablespoons olive oil
1 large onion, diced
3 cloves garlic, finely chopped
1 small red capsicum, thinly sliced
1 small red chilli, seeded and chopped
2 teaspoons paprika
1 teaspoon ground turmeric
2 tomatoes, peeled and diced

1 tablespoon tomato paste
2 cups (400 g/12 oz) long-grain rice
½ cup (125 ml/4 fl oz) white wine
5 cups (1.25 litres) fish stock
3 tablespoons chopped fresh flat-leaf parsley,
for serving
lemon wedges, for serving

PREPARATION TIME 25 minutes
TOTAL COOKING TIME 45 minutes
SERVES 6

1 Peel the prawns, leaving the tails intact. Gently pull out the dark vein from each prawn back, starting at the head end. Cut the fish fillets into cubes. Scrub the mussels and pull out the hairy beards. Discard any broken mussels or any that don't close when tapped. Refrigerate the seafood, covered, until ready to use.

2 Heat the oil in a paella pan or a large deep frying pan with a lid. Add the onion, garlic, capsicum and chilli to the pan and cook over medium heat for 2 minutes, or until the onion and capsicum are soft. Add the paprika, turmeric and 1 teaspoon salt and stir-fry for 1–2 minutes, or until aromatic.

3 Add the tomato and cook for 5 minutes, or until softened. Add the tomato paste. Stir in the rice until it is well coated.

4 Pour in the wine and simmer until almost absorbed. Add all the fish stock and bring to the boil. Reduce the heat and simmer until almost all the liquid is absorbed into the rice. Occasionally fluff the rice up with a fork.

5 Add the mussels to the pan, poking the shells into the rice, cover and cook for 2–3 minutes over low heat. Add the prawns and cook for 2–3 minutes. Add the fish, cover and cook for 3 minutes. Finally, add the calamari rings and cook for 1–2 minutes. By this time, the mussels should have opened—discard any unopened ones. Cook for another 2–3 minutes if the seafood is not quite cooked, but avoid over-cooking as the seafood will toughen and dry out.

6 Serve with parsley and lemon wedges and a green salad.

NUTRITION PER SERVE Protein 44.5 g; **Fat 14.5 g**; Carbohydrate 60 g; Dietary Fibre 3.5 g; Cholesterol 217 mg; 2360 kJ (560 cal)

Swordfish Kebabs with Roast Potatoes

600 g (1¼ lb) potatoes, cut in half
olive oil, for brushing
2 cloves garlic, crushed
1 red onion, cut into 8 wedges
1 red capsicum, cut into cubes
2 zucchini, cut into pieces
1 kg (2 lb) swordfish, cut into cubes

bay leaves, torn in half
1 tablespoon olive oil, extra
1 tablespoon lemon juice

PREPARATION TIME 40 minutes
TOTAL COOKING TIME 1 hour
SERVES 4

1 Preheat the oven to moderately hot 190°C (375°F/Gas 5). Brush the potatoes with olive oil and place cut-side-up in a baking dish. Bake for 40 minutes, or until crisp.

2 Preheat a lightly oiled chargrill pan or barbecue flatplate. Add the garlic, onion and capsicum and cook, stirring, for 5 minutes. Toss in the zucchini and cook for a further 5 minutes, or until the vegetables are tender. Remove from the heat and season.

3 Thread the swordfish cubes onto 8 metal skewers, interspersed with the bay leaves. Lightly coat with olive oil and the lemon juice.

4 Reheat and lightly oil the hot plate and cook the kebabs for about 4 minutes, turning frequently. Arrange the vegetables on 4 warm plates, top with the kebabs and serve the potatoes on the side.

NUTRITION PER SERVE Protein 57 g; **Fat 12 g**; Carbohydrate 22.5 g; Dietary Fibre 4 g; Cholesterol 175 mg; 1805 kJ (430 cal)

Glazed Grilled Fish

2 tablespoons olive oil
2 tablespoons lemon juice
2 tablespoons fruit chutney
1 tablespoon honey
2 small cloves garlic, crushed
4 firm white fish fillets (ling or perch)

PREPARATION TIME 15 minutes + 10 minutes marinating
TOTAL COOKING TIME 10 minutes
SERVES 4

1 Combine the oil, lemon juice, chutney, honey and garlic in a small jug.

2 Place the fish in a non-metallic flat dish and cover with the oil mixture. Marinate for 10 minutes

3 Transfer the fish to a lightly greased grill tray, reserving the marinade. Cook under a hot grill for 4 minutes each side or until tender, occasionally brushing with the reserved marinade. Serve with steamed vegetables and a wedge of lemon.

NUTRITION PER SERVE Protein 14 g; **Fat 11 g**; Carbohydrate 10 g; Dietary Fibre 0.5 g; cholesterol 46 mg; 831 kJ (198 cal)

Japanese-style Salmon Parcels

2 teaspoons sesame seeds
4 x 150 g (5 oz) salmon
cutlets or steaks
2.5 cm (1 inch) piece ginger
2 celery sticks
4 spring onions
¼ teaspoon dashi granules

3 tablespoons mirin
2 tablespoons tamari

PREPARATION TIME 40 minutes
TOTAL COOKING TIME 15 minutes
SERVES 4

1 Cut baking paper into four squares large enough to enclose the salmon steaks. Preheat the oven to very hot 230°C (450°F/Gas 8). Lightly toast the sesame seeds.

2 Wash the salmon and dry with paper towels. Place a salmon cutlet in the centre of each paper square.

3 Cut the ginger into paper-thin slices. Slice the celery and spring onions into short lengths, then lengthways into fine strips. Arrange a bundle of the prepared strips and several slices of ginger on each salmon steak.

4 Combine the dashi granules, mirin and tamari in a small saucepan. Heat gently until the granules dissolve. Drizzle over each parcel, sprinkle with sesame seeds and carefully wrap the salmon, folding in the sides to seal in all the juices. Arrange the parcels on a baking tray and cook for about 12 minutes, or until tender. (The paper will puff up when the fish is cooked.) Do not overcook or the salmon will dry out. Serve immediately, as standing time can spoil the fish.

Note
Dashi, mirin and tamari are all available from Japanese food stores.

NUTRITION PER SERVE Protein 20 g; **Fat 14 g**; Carbohydrate 0 g; Dietary Fibre 0.5 g; Cholesterol 85 mg; 935 kJ (225 cal)

Spicy Chicken Patties

500 g (1 lb) chicken mince
4 spring onions, finely chopped
$1/3$ cup (20 g/$3/4$ oz) finely chopped fresh
coriander leaves
2 cloves garlic, crushed
$3/4$ teaspoon cayenne pepper
1 egg white, lightly beaten

1 tablespoon oil
1 lemon, halved

PREPARATION TIME 10 minutes + 20 minutes
refrigeration
TOTAL COOKING TIME 10 minutes
SERVES 4

1 Preheat the oven to warm 170°C (325°F/Gas 2–3). Mix together all the ingredients except the oil and lemon, season with salt and pepper and shape the mixture into 4 patties. Refrigerate for 20 minutes before cooking.

2 Heat the oil in a large frying pan over medium heat, add the patties and cook for about 5 minutes on each side, or until browned and cooked through.

3 Squeeze the lemon on the cooked patties and drain well on paper towels. Serve with a salad or use to make burgers with crusty rolls.

NUTRITION PER SERVE Protein 25 g; **Fat 12 g**; Carbohydrate 1 g; Dietary Fibre 1 g; Cholesterol 105 mg; 895 kJ (215 cal)

Lime Steamed Chicken

2 limes, thinly sliced
4 chicken breast fillets
1 bunch (500 g/1 lb) bok choy
1 bunch (500 g/1 lb) choy sum
1 teaspoon sesame oil
1 tablespoon peanut oil

$^1/_2$ cup (125 ml/4 fl oz) oyster sauce
$^1/_3$ cup (80 ml/2$^3/_4$ fl oz) lime juice

PREPARATION TIME 15 minutes
TOTAL COOKING TIME 15 minutes
SERVES 4

1 Line the base of a bamboo steamer with the lime, place the chicken on top and season. Place over a wok with a little water in the base, cover and steam for 8–10 minutes, or until the chicken is cooked through. Cover the chicken and keep warm. Remove the water from the wok.

2 Wash and trim the greens. Heat the oils in the wok and cook the greens for 2–3 minutes, or until just wilted.

3 Combine the oyster sauce and lime juice and pour over the greens when they are cooked. Place the chicken on serving plates on top of the greens and serve with rice and lime slices.

Note
The Asian green vegetables used in this recipe, bok choy and choy sum, can be replaced by any green vegetables, such as broccoli, snow peas, or English spinach.

NUTRITION PER SERVE Protein 60 g; **Fat 12 g**; Carbohydrate 10 g; Dietary Fibre 4.5 g; Cholesterol 120 mg; 1665 kJ (398 cal)

Saffron Chicken

1 teaspoon saffron threads
2 tablespoons hot water
2 tablespoons oil
2 onions, chopped
3 cloves garlic, crushed
3 cm (1 1/4 inch) piece ginger, chopped
2 red chillies, seeded and sliced
1 teaspoon ground cardamom

1 teaspoon ground cumin
1/2 teaspoon ground turmeric
2 kg (4 lb) chicken pieces
2 cups (500 ml/16 fl oz) chicken stock

PREPARATION TIME 25 minutes
TOTAL COOKING TIME 1 hour 20 minutes
SERVES 6

1 Fry the saffron threads in a dry frying pan over low heat for 1–2 minutes. Transfer to a small bowl, add the hot water and set aside.

2 Heat the oil in a pan over medium heat. Add the onion, garlic, ginger and chilli. Cover and cook for 10 minutes, or until very soft.

3 Add the cardamom, cumin and turmeric, and cook over medium heat for 2 minutes. Add the chicken pieces and cook over high heat for 3 minutes, or until the meat is well coated. Add the saffron liquid and the chicken stock. Bring to the boil, then reduce the heat and cook, covered, stirring occasionally, for 30 minutes.

4 Uncover, and cook for a further 20 minutes. Remove the chicken and keep warm. Reduce the stock to about 1 1/2 cups (375 ml/12 fl oz) over very high heat. Pour over the chicken. Season with salt and pepper, to taste.

NUTRITION PER SERVE Protein 45 g; **Fat 15 g**; Carbohydrate 3 g; Dietary Fibre 1 g; Cholesterol 155 mg; 1445 kJ (345 cal)

Sichuan Pepper Chicken Stir-fry

3 teaspoons Sichuan pepper
500 g (1 lb) chicken thigh fillets, cut into strips
2 tablespoons soy sauce
1 clove garlic, crushed
1 teaspoon grated fresh ginger
3 teaspoons cornflour
100 g (3½ oz) dried thin egg noodles
oil, for cooking
1 onion, sliced

1 yellow capsicum, cut into thin strips
1 red capsicum, cut into thin strips
100 g (3½ oz) sugar snap peas
¼ cup (60 ml/2 fl oz) chicken stock

PREPARATION TIME 25 minutes + 2 hours marinating
TOTAL COOKING TIME 20 minutes
SERVES 4

1 Heat the wok until very hot and dry-fry the Sichuan pepper for 30 seconds. Remove from the wok and crush with a mortar and pestle.

2 Combine the chicken with the soy sauce, garlic, ginger, cornflour and Sichuan pepper in a non-metallic bowl. Cover and refrigerate for 2 hours.

3 Cook the noodles in a large saucepan of boiling water for 5 minutes, or until tender. Drain, then drizzle with a little oil and toss it through the noodles to prevent them from sticking together. Set aside.

4 Heat the wok until very hot, add 1 tablespoon oil and swirl to coat. Stir-fry the chicken in batches over medium–high heat for 5 minutes, or until golden brown and cooked. Add more oil when necessary. Remove from the wok.

5 Reheat the wok, add 1 tablespoon oil and stir-fry the onion, capsicum and peas over high heat for 2–3 minutes, or until tender. Add the chicken stock and bring to the boil. Return the chicken and egg noodles to the wok and toss over high heat until well combined. Serve immediately.

NUTRITION PER SERVE Protein 35 g; **Fat 15 g**; Carbohydrate 25 g; Dietary Fibre 3 g; Cholesterol 65 mg; 1515 kJ (360 cal)

Chicken Chasseur

1 kg (2 lb) chicken thigh fillets
1 tablespoon oil
1 clove garlic, crushed
1 large onion, sliced
100 g (3½ oz) button mushrooms, sliced
1 teaspoon thyme leaves
400 g (13 oz) can chopped tomatoes

¼ cup (60 ml/2 fl oz) chicken stock
¼ cup (60 ml/2 fl oz) white wine
1 tablespoon tomato paste

PREPARATION TIME 20 minutes
TOTAL COOKING TIME 1 hour 30 minutes
SERVES 4

1 Preheat the oven to moderate 180°C (350°F/Gas 4) Trim the chicken of any fat and sinew. Heat the oil in a heavy-based frying pan and brown the chicken in batches over medium heat. Drain on paper towels and then transfer to a casserole dish.

2 Add the garlic, onion and mushrooms to the pan and cook over medium heat for 5 minutes, or until soft. Add to the chicken with the thyme and tomatoes.

3 Combine the stock, wine and tomato paste and pour over the chicken. Cover and bake for 1¼ hours, or until the chicken is tender and cooked through.

Hint
Best cooked a day in advance to let the flavours develop.

NUTRITION PER SERVE Protein 60 g; **Fat 12 g**; Carbohydrate 6 g; Dietary Fibre 2 g; Cholesterol 125 mg; 1710 kJ (410 cal)

Pork and Tomato Burgers

350 g (11 1/2 oz) pork and veal mince
100 g (3 1/2 oz) sun-dried tomatoes, chopped
3 spring onions, finely chopped
2 tablespoons chopped fresh basil
1 red capsicum, seeded and sliced
olive oil for cooking
1 tablespoon balsamic vinegar

PREPARATION TIME 20 minutes + 15 minutes refrigeration
TOTAL COOKING TIME 15 minutes
SERVES 4

1 Combine the pork and veal mince, sun-dried tomato, spring onion, basil and salt and pepper in a bowl. Knead for 2 minutes, or until the meat becomes a little sticky. Form into 4 patties and refrigerate for 15 minutes.

2 Mix the capsicum with a little olive oil. Cook on a preheated chargrill pan or barbeque flatplate, tossing well and drizzling with the balsamic vinegar until just softened. Remove and set aside.

3 Wipe the flatplate clean and reheat. Brush the patties with a little olive oil and cook for about 4–5 minutes each side, or until browned and cooked through. Serve with the chargrilled capsicum.

NUTRITION PER SERVE Protein 20 g; **Fat 10 g**; Carbohydrate 5 g; Dietary Fibre 2 g; Cholesterol 45 mg; 840 kJ (200 cal)

Pork with Snake Beans

oil, for cooking
400 g (13 oz) pork fillet, cut into thick slices
2 onions, thinly sliced
150 g (5 oz) snake beans, diagonally sliced
(see NOTE)
3 cloves garlic, finely chopped
1 tablespoon finely chopped
fresh ginger

1 red capsicum, thinly sliced
6 spring onions, diagonally sliced
2 tablespoons sweet chilli sauce

PREPARATION TIME 15 minutes
TOTAL COOKING TIME 20 minutes
SERVES 4

1 Heat the wok until very hot, add 2 teaspoons of the oil and swirl it around to coat the side. Stir-fry the pork in two batches over high heat for 3–4 minutes, or until it is just cooked, adding more oil when necessary. Remove all the pork from the wok.

2 Heat 1 tablespoon of the oil over medium heat and add the sliced onion. Cook for 3–4 minutes, or until the onion has softened slightly. Add the sliced snake beans and cook for 2–3 minutes. Add the garlic, ginger, capsicum and spring onion, and toss well. Increase the heat and cook for 3–4 minutes.

3 Return the pork to the wok, add the sweet chilli sauce and toss well. Remove from the heat and season with salt and pepper. Serve immediately.

Note
If you can't find snake beans you can use ordinary green beans in this recipe.

NUTRITION PER SERVE Protein 25 g; **Fat 12 g**; Carbohydrate 8 g; Dietary Fibre 4 g; Cholesterol 50 mg; 1005 kJ (240 cal)

Pork with Rice Stick Noodles

150 g (5 oz) rice stick noodles
2 tablespoons oil
200 g (6$\frac{1}{2}$ oz) pork eye fillet, thinly sliced
3 cloves garlic, crushed
1 carrot, cut into matchsticks
50 g (1$\frac{1}{2}$ oz) snow peas, cut lengthways into matchsticks
1 tablespoon soy sauce
1 tablespoon lime juice

2 teaspoons soft brown sugar
1 teaspoon fish sauce
1 tablespoon chopped fresh chives
1 tablespoon chopped fresh mint

PREPARATION TIME 15 minutes + 10 minutes soaking
TOTAL COOKING TIME 15 minutes
SERVES 4

1 Soak the noodles in boiling water for 5–10 minutes, or until they are soft. Drain and set aside on a clean tea towel to dry.

2 Meanwhile, heat 1 tablespoon of the oil in a wok or heavy-based frying pan. When the oil is hot, fry the pork slices and garlic, in batches, until the pork is cooked through and browned. (Add more oil if necessary.) Remove, set aside and keep warm.

3 Heat the remaining oil in the wok or frying pan and stir-fry the carrot and snow peas for 2–3 minutes over high heat. Return the pork slices to the wok along with the noodles and toss everything together.

4 Add the soy sauce, lime juice, brown sugar and fish sauce. Toss together until well combined.

5 Before serving, add the chopped chives and mint and mix together well.

NUTRITION PER SERVE Protein 15 g; **Fat 10 g**; Carbohydrate 15 g; Dietary Fibre 2 g; Cholesterol 30 mg; 935 kJ (225 cal)

Pork and Mustard Stew

2 tablespoons oil
1 kg (2 lb) pork neck, cut into 3 cm
(1¼ inch) cubes
20 g (½ oz) butter
1 large onion, sliced
1 clove garlic, crushed
250 g (8 oz) button mushrooms, halved
1 tablespoon plain flour
⅓ cup (80 ml) lemon juice

1 cup (250 ml) chicken stock
2 tablespoons wholegrain mustard
2 teaspoons honey
½ teaspoon ground cumin

PREPARATION TIME 15 minutes
TOTAL COOKING TIME 1 hour 10 minutes
SERVES 4–6

1 Preheat the oven to warm 170°C (325°F/Gas 3). Heat the oil in a large saucepan and brown the pork in batches over high heat. Transfer to a large casserole dish.

2 Add the butter to the pan and cook the onion and garlic until soft but not brown. Add the mushrooms and cook for 1 minute. Stir in the flour, then the remaining ingredients. Bring to the boil, stirring. Season to taste and spoon the mixture over the pork. Cover and bake for 45 minutes, or until tender.

NUTRITION PER SERVE Protein 40 g; **Fat 10 g**; Carbohydrate 5 g; Dietary Fibre 2 g; Cholesterol 85 mg; 1195 kJ (285 cal)

Lamb Cutlets with Tomato and Spinach sauce

2 tablespoons olive oil
1 onion, chopped
2 clover garlic, chopped
425 g (14 oz) can chopped tomatoes
2 tablespoons red wine
8 lamb cutlets
1 tablespoon sun-dried tomato pesto

PREPARATION TIME 10 minutes
TOTAL COOKING TIME 25 minutes
SERVES 4

1 Heat the oil in a saucepan and add the onion and garlic. Cover and cook over medium heat for 3 minutes, or until the onion is soft. Add the undrained tomatoes and the red wine and simmer for 10 minutes.

2 Trim the excess fat from the lamb cutlets and season with salt and freshly ground black pepper. Place under a hot grill and cook for 3 minutes on each side, or until cooked to your liking. Cover and leave in a warm place.

3 Stir the pesto and spinach into the tomato sauce and cook for 1 minute. Drizzle the sauce over the cutlets. Boiled baby potatoes make a delicious accompaniment to this meal.

NUTRITION PER SERVE Protein 20 g; **Fat 15 g**; Carbohydrate 5.5 g; Dietary Fibre 3 g; Cholesterol 48 mg; 956 kj (230 cal)

Tagine of Lamb with Quince and Lemon

1.5 kg (3 lb) boned shoulder of lamb, cut into
12 even pieces
1 onion, finely chopped
2 cloves garlic, crushed
1 cinnamon stick
1 teaspoon ground ginger
1/2 teaspoon saffron threads
1 large quince, peeled, seeded and cut into
12 pieces

1/4 cup (90 ml/3 fl oz) honey
1 teaspoon ground cinnamon
1/2 preserved lemon

PREPARATION TIME 25 minutes
TOTAL COOKING TIME 2 hours 10 minutes
SERVES 4

1 Trim the lamb of excess fat and place in a large pan. Add the onion, garlic, cinnamon stick, ginger and saffron and enough cold water to cover. Slowly bring to the boil, stirring occasionally. Reduce the heat, cover and simmer for 45 minutes. Transfer the meat to a casserole dish.

2 Add the quince, honey and ground cinnamon to the cooking liquid and simmer for 15 minutes, or until the quince is tender. Discard the cinnamon, remove the quince and add to the meat, reserving the liquid.

3 Preheat the oven to moderate 180°C (350°F/Gas 4). Boil the cooking liquid for 30 minutes, or until reduced by half, then pour over the meat and quince. Remove and discard the flesh from the lemon. Slice the rind thinly, then add to the meat. Cover and bake for 40 minutes, or until the meat is tender.

Hint
As you work, place the peeled quince in water with a little lemon juice to prevent discolouring.

NUTRITION PER SERVE Protein 80 g; **Fat 15 g**; Carbohydrate 20 g; Dietary Fibre 3 g; Cholesterol 250 mg; 2160 kJ (515 cal)

Rogan Josh

1 kg (2 lb) boned leg of lamb
1 tablespoon oil
2 onions, chopped
½ cup (125 g/4 oz) low-fat natural yoghurt
1 teaspoon chilli powder
1 tablespoon ground coriander
2 teaspoons ground cumin
1 teaspoon ground cardamom
½ teaspoon ground cloves
1 teaspoon ground turmeric

3 cloves garlic, crushed
1 tablespoon grated fresh ginger
400 g (13 oz) can chopped tomatoes
¼ cup (30 g/1 oz) slivered almonds
1 teaspoon garam masala
chopped fresh coriander leaves, for serving

PREPARATION TIME 25 minutes
TOTAL COOKING TIME 1 hour 40 minutes
SERVES 6

1 Trim the lamb of any fat or sinew and cut into small cubes.

2 Heat the oil in a large saucepan, add the onion and cook, stirring, for 5 minutes, or until soft. Stir in the yoghurt, chilli powder, coriander, cumin, cardamom, cloves, turmeric, garlic and ginger. Add the tomato and 1 teaspoon salt and simmer for 5 minutes.

3 Add the lamb and stir until coated. Cover and cook over low heat, stirring occasionally, for 1–1½ hours, or until the lamb is tender. Uncover and simmer until the liquid thickens.

4 Meanwhile, toast the almonds in a dry frying pan over medium heat for 3–4 minutes, shaking the pan gently, until the nuts are golden brown. Remove from the pan at once to prevent them burning.

5 Add the garam masala to the curry and mix through well. Sprinkle the slivered almonds and coriander leaves over the top and serve.

NUTRITION PER SERVE Protein 40 g; **Fat 13 g**; Carbohydrate 5.5 g; Dietary Fibre 2 g; Cholesterol 122 mg; 1236 kJ (295 cal)

Moussaka

1 kg (2 lb) eggplants
cooking oil spray
400 g (13 oz) lean lamb mince
2 onions, finely chopped
2 cloves garlic, crushed
400 g (13 oz) can tomatoes
1 tablespoon chopped fresh thyme
1 teaspoon chopped fresh oregano
1 tablespoon tomato paste
1/3 cup (80 ml/2 3/4 fl oz) dry white wine
1 bay leaf
1 teaspoon sugar

Cheese sauce
1 1/4 cups (315 ml/10 fl oz) skim milk
2 tablespoons plain flour
1/4 cup (30 g/1 oz) grated reduced-fat Cheddar
1 cup (250 g/8 oz) ricotta
pinch of cayenne pepper
1/4 teaspoon ground nutmeg

PREPARATION TIME 30 minutes
TOTAL COOKING TIME 1 hour 30 minutes
SERVES 6

1 Cut the eggplant into 1 cm (1/2 inch) thick slices, place in a colander over a large bowl, layering with a generous sprinkling of salt, and leave to stand for 20 minutes. This is to draw out the bitter juices.

2 Lightly spray a non-stick frying pan with oil and brown the lamb mince, over medium-high heat. Once all the meat is browned, set aside.

3 Spray the pan again with oil, add the onion and stir continuously for 2 minutes. Add 1 tablespoon water to the pan to prevent sticking. Add the garlic and cook until the onion is golden brown.

4 Push the undrained tomatoes through a sieve, then discard the contents of the sieve.

5 Return the meat to the pan with the onion. Add the herbs, tomato pulp, tomato paste, wine, bay leaf and sugar. Cover and simmer over low heat for 20 minutes. Preheat a grill.

6 Thoroughly rinse and pat dry the eggplant, place on a grill tray, spray lightly with oil and grill under high heat until golden brown. Turn over, spray lightly with oil and grill until golden brown. Arrange half the eggplant slices over the base of a 1.5 litre capacity baking dish. Top with half the meat mixture and then repeat the layers.

7 Preheat the oven to moderate 180°C (350°F/Gas 4). To make the sauce, blend a little of the milk with the flour to form a paste in a small pan. Gradually blend in the remaining milk, stirring constantly over low heat until the milk starts to simmer and thicken. Remove from the heat and stir in the Cheddar, ricotta, cayenne and nutmeg. Pour over the moussaka and bake for until the cheese is golden brown and the moussaka heated through.

NUTRITION PER SERVE Protein 10 g; **Fat 10 g**; Carbohydrate 15 g; Dietary Fibre 5.5 g; Cholesterol 25 mg;735 kJ (175 cal)

Beef Kebabs with Mint Yoghurt Dressing

½ cup (125 ml/4 fl oz) olive oil
⅓ cup (80 ml/2¾ fl oz) lemon juice
1 tablespoon chopped fresh rosemary
500 g (1 lb) lean beef fillet, cubed
1 red onion, cut into wedges
200 g (6½ oz) slender eggplants, sliced

Dressing
1 cup (250 g) plain yoghurt
1 clove garlic, crushed
1 small Lebanese cucumber, grated
2 tablespoons chopped fresh mint

PREPARATION TIME 30 minutes + 2 hours marinating
TOTAL COOKING TIME 10 minutes
MAKES 8

1 Soak 8 wooden skewers in cold water for 30 minutes. Combine the olive oil, lemon juice and rosemary and pour over the beef, coating thoroughly. Cover and refrigerate for 2 hours.

2 To make the mint yoghurt dressing, combine the yoghurt, garlic, cucumber and mint and season with salt and ground black pepper to taste.

3 Thread the drained beef alternately with the onion wedges and slices of eggplant onto the wooden skewers.

4 Preheat a lightly oiled chargrill pan or barbecue grill or flatplate. Cook the kebabs over high heat, turning regularly, for 5–10 minutes, or until the beef is cooked through and tender. Serve with the mint yoghurt dressing.

NUTRITION PER KEBAB Protein 15 g; **Fat 15 g**; Carbohydrate 3 g; Dietary Fibre 1 g; Cholesterol 40 mg; 1010 kJ (240 cal)

Beef with Oyster Sauce

1 ½ teaspoons cornflour
½ cup (125 ml/4 fl oz) beef stock
2 tablespoons oyster sauce
1 teaspoon finely crushed garlic
1 teaspoon caster sugar
oil, for cooking
350 g (12 oz) rump steak, finely sliced
250 g (8 oz) beans, topped and tailed, cut into
5 cm (2 inch) lengths

1 small red capsicum, sliced
½ cup (60 g/2 oz) bean sprouts

PREPARATION TIME 15 minutes
TOTAL COOKING TIME 5 minutes
SERVES 4

1 Dissolve the cornflour in a little of the stock. Mix with the remaining stock, oyster sauce, garlic and sugar and set aside.

2 Heat the wok until very hot, add 1 tablespoon of the oil and swirl it around to coat the side. Add the beef in batches and stir-fry over high heat for 2 minutes, or until it browns.

3 Add the beans and capsicum and stir-fry another minute.

4 Add the cornflour mixture to the wok and cook until the sauce boils and thickens. Stir in the bean sprouts and serve immediately.

NUTRITION PER SERVE Protein 23 g; **Fat 12 g**; Carbohydrate 10 g; Dietary Fibre 2.5 g; Cholesterol 60 mg; 1016 kJ (243 cal)

Stir-fried Fresh Rice Noodles with Beef

2 cloves garlic, crushed
2 teaspoons finely chopped
fresh ginger
1 tablespoon oyster sauce
2 teaspoons soy sauce
500 g (1 lb) sliced beef
¼ cup (60 ml/2 fl oz) oil
1 kg (2 lb) fresh rice noodles, sliced into
2 cm strips

100 g (3½ oz) fresh garlic chives, chopped
2½ tablespoons oyster sauce, extra
3 teaspoons soy sauce, extra
1 teaspoon sugar

PREPARATION TIME 10 minutes + 30 minutes
marinating
TOTAL COOKING TIME 15 minutes
SERVES 4–6

1 Combine the garlic, ginger, oyster and soy sauces, add the beef and toss to coat. Cover and refrigerate for 30 minutes.

2 Heat a wok until very hot, add 1 tablespoon oil and swirl to coat. Add half the beef and stir-fry for 5 minutes, or until cooked. Remove and repeat with the remaining beef. Add the remaining oil, then the noodles and stir-fry for 3–5 minutes, or until softened.

3 Add the garlic chives, and stir-fry until just wilted. Stir in the extra oyster and soy sauces, and sugar, return the beef to the wok and toss to heat through.

NUTRITION PER SERVE Protein 33 g; **Fat 13 g**; Carbohydrate 40 g; Dietary Fibre 1.5 g; Cholesterol 50 mg; 1295 kJ (310 cal)

Lasagne

2 teaspoons olive oil
1 large onion, chopped
2 carrots, finely chopped
2 celery sticks, finely chopped
2 zucchini, finely chopped
2 cloves garlic, crushed
500 g (1 lb) lean beef mince
2 x 400 g (13 oz) cans crushed tomatoes
1/2 cup (125 ml/4 fl oz) beef stock
2 tablespoons tomato paste

2 teaspoons dried oregano
375 g (12 oz) instant or fresh lasagne sheets

Cheese sauce
1/3 cup (40 g/1 1/4 oz) cornflour
3 cups (750 ml/24 fl oz) skim milk
100 g (3 1/2 oz) reduced-fat cheese, grated

PREPARATION TIME 40 minutes
TOTAL COOKING TIME 1 hour 35 minutes
SERVES 8

1 Heat the olive oil in a large non-stick frying pan. Add the onion and cook for 5 minutes, until soft. Add the carrot, celery and zucchini and cook, stirring constantly, for 5 minutes, or until the vegetables are soft. Add the crushed garlic and cook for another minute. Add the beef mince and cook over high heat, stirring, until well browned.

2 Add the crushed tomato, beef stock, tomato paste and dried oregano to the pan and stir to combine. Bring the mixture to the boil, then reduce the heat and simmer gently, partially covered, for 20 minutes, stirring occasionally to prevent sticking.

3 Preheat the oven to moderate 180°C (350°F/Gas 4). Spread a little of the meat sauce into the base of a 23 x 30 cm (9 x 12 inch) ovenproof dish. Arrange a layer of lasagne sheets in the dish, breaking some of the sheets, if necessary, to fit in neatly.

4 Spread half the meat sauce over the top to cover evenly. Cover with another layer of lasagne sheets, a layer of meat sauce, then a final layer of lasagne sheets.

5 To make the cheese sauce, blend a little of the milk with the cornflour, to form a smooth paste, in a small pan. Gradually blend in the remaining milk and stir constantly over low heat until the mixture boils and thickens. Remove from the heat and stir in the grated cheese until melted. Spread evenly over the top of the lasagne and bake for 1 hour.

6 Check the lasagne after 25 minutes. If the top is browning too quickly, cover loosely with non-stick baking paper or foil. Take care when removing the baking paper or foil that the topping does not come away with the paper. For serving, cut the lasagne into eight portions and garnish with fresh herbs.

NUTRITION PER SERVE Protein 15 g; **Fat 12 g**; Carbohydrate 50 g; Dietary Fibre 5 g; Cholesterol 10 mg; 1885 kJ (450 cal)

Lime and Blueberry Tart

375 g (12 oz) sweet shortcrust pastry
3 eggs
½ cup (125 g/4 oz) caster sugar
¼ cup (60 ml/2 fl oz) buttermilk
1 tablespoon lime juice
2 teaspoons finely grated lime rind

2 tablespoons custard powder
250 g (8 oz) blueberries

PREPARATION TIME 30 minutes + 20 minutes
refrigeration
TOTAL COOKING TIME 1 hour
SERVES 8

1 Roll out the pastry between two sheets of baking paper to line a 22 cm (9 inch) pie tin, trimming away the excess. Refrigerate for 20 minutes.

2 Preheat the oven to 200°C (400°F/Gas 6). Line the pastry with baking paper and spread with baking beads or rice. Bake for 10 minutes, remove the paper and beads and bake for 4–5 minutes, or until the pastry is dry. Cool slightly. Reduce the oven to 180°C (350°F/Gas 4).

3 To make the filling, beat the eggs and caster sugar with electric beaters until thick and pale. Add the buttermilk, lime juice and rind, and sifted custard powder. Stir together, then spoon into the pastry shell. Bake for 15 minutes, then reduce the oven to 160°C (315°F/Gas 2–3) and cook for another 20–25 minutes, or until the filling has coloured slightly and is set. Leave to cool (the filling will sink a little), then top with the blueberries.

NUTRITION PER SERVE Protein 5.5 g; **Fat 14 g**; Carbohydrate 38.5 g; Dietary Fibre 1 g; Cholesterol 81.5 mg; 1240 kJ (295 cal)

Hot Chocolate Soufflé

170 g (5½ oz) caster sugar
450 ml (16 fl oz) milk
70 g (2¼ oz) plain flour
1 egg
4 eggs, separated
40 g (1¼ oz) butter, melted
¼ cup (30 g/1 oz) cocoa powder, sifted

1 tablespoon caster sugar, extra
icing sugar, to serve

PREPARATION TIME 20 minutes + cooling
TOTAL COOKING TIME 35 minutes
SERVES 8

1 Grease a 1.25 litre (44 fl oz) soufflé dish and preheat the oven to moderately hot 200°C (400°F/Gas 6).

2 Put the sugar and 1 cup (250 ml) milk in a pan and stir over low heat until the sugar dissolves. Put the flour, egg and the remaining milk in a bowl and whisk to combine. Pour the hot milk mixture into the bowl and mix well with a whisk. When smooth, return the mixture to the pan and stir over low heat until it boils and thickens. Combine the egg yolks and butter with the cocoa and add to the pan, mixing well. Transfer to a bowl, cover the surface with plastic wrap and allow to cool completely.

3 In a large clean dry bowl, beat the egg whites until soft peaks form, then add the extra sugar. Continue beating until well combined and the egg whites are glossy. Carefully combine one spoonful of the egg whites with the chocolate mixture, then add the remaining egg white and fold in gently with a metal spoon. Fill the soufflé dish to three-quarters full and place on an oven tray. Bake for 25–30 minutes, or until puffed up and firm to the touch. Dust with icing sugar before serving.

NUTRITION PER SERVE Protein 7.5 g; **Fat 10 g**; Carbohydrate 35 g; Dietary Fibre 0.5 g; Cholesterol 135 mg; 1065 kJ (255 cal)

Toffee Puddings

canola oil spray
60 g (2 oz) reduced-fat dairy spread
100 g (3½ oz) caster sugar
1 egg
3 teaspoons grated orange rind
100 g (3½ oz) self-raising flour
½ teaspoon baking powder

½ cup (175 g/5½ oz) golden syrup
100 ml (3½ fl oz) orange juice

PREPARATION TIME 15 minutes
TOTAL COOKING TIME 20 minutes
SERVES 4

1 Preheat the oven to warm 170°C (325°F/Gas 3). Lightly spray four ½ cup (125 ml) ovenproof ramekins with canola oil.

2 Cream the dairy spread with 80 g (2½ oz) caster sugar until light and fluffy. Add the egg and half the orange rind, and mix together until well combined.

3 Sift the flour and baking powder together, then fold into the creamed mixture until it is quite thick.

4 Mix 2 tablespoons golden syrup with the remaining orange rind and fold through the creamed mixture. Divide among the ramekins and bake for 15–20 minutes, or until firm to the touch.

5 Meanwhile, place the orange juice and remaining sugar and golden syrup in a saucepan and bring to the boil over high heat. Cook for 5 minutes, or until slightly thickened. Strain to remove any scum, then remove the puddings from the dishes and spoon the sauce over the top. Serve with low-fat whipped cream or yoghurt, if desired.

NUTRITION PER SERVE Protein 5 g; **Fat 10 g**; Carbohydrate 78 g; Dietary Fibre 1 g; Cholesterol 61.5 mg; 1715 kJ (410 cal)

Bread and Butter Pudding

30 g (1 oz) butter, softened
6 thin slices day-old bread, crusts removed
¾ cup (140 g/4¼ oz) mixed dried fruit
¼ cup (60 g/2 oz) caster sugar
1 teaspoon mixed spice
2 eggs, lightly beaten

1 teaspoon vanilla essence
2½ cups (625 ml/22 fl oz) milk

PREPARATION TIME 10 minutes
TOTAL COOKING TIME 50 minutes
SERVES 4–6

1 Preheat the oven to moderate 180°C (350°F/ Gas 4). Grease a shallow ovenproof dish. Butter the bread and halve diagonally. Layer the bread in the dish, sprinkling each layer with the fruit, sugar and spice.

2 Beat the eggs, vanilla and milk together. Pour over the bread and leave for 5 minutes. Bake the pudding for 40–50 minutes, or until it is set and the top is browned.

NUTRITION PER SERVE Protein 9 g; **Fat 10 g**; Carbohydrate 45 g; Dietary Fibre 2 g; Cholesterol 90 mg; 1260 kJ (300 cal)

Index

First published in 2004 by Murdoch Books Pty Limited,
Pier 8/9, 23 Hickson Road, Millers Point, NSW 2000,
AUSTRALIA
Phone: + 61 (0) 2 8220 2000   Fax: + 61 (0) 2 8220 2558

Murdoch Books UK Ltd, Erico House, 6th Floor North,
93-99 Upper Richmond Road, Putney, London SW15 2TG.
Phone: + 44 (0) 20 8355 1480   Fax: + 44 (0) 20 8355 1499

Editor: Anouska Jones
Design: Jenny Cowan
Production Controller: Monika Paratore

ISBN 1 74045 489 8.

A catalogue record of this book is available from the
National Library of Australia.

Printed by Midas (Asia) Ltd. PRINTED IN CHINA.
Reprinted 2005.

Also available in this series:
*The low carb cookbook,
low carb not no carb*
ISBN: 1-74045-393-X